# *Lighten Your Mental Load*

*Amy Thornton*

**Lighten Your Mental Load**

Lighten Your Mental Load ©2019, by Amy Shankland
Wise Words Publishing, an affiliate of Tell-Tale Publishing Group, LLC
Swartz Creek, MI  48473

Tell-Tale Publishing Group and its affiliates supports the right to free expression and the value of copyright. The purpose of copyright is to encourage writers and artists to produce the creative works that enrich our culture. The scanning, uploading, and distribution of this book without permission is a theft of the author's intellectual property. If you would like permission to use material from the book (other than for review purposes), please contact:

permissions@tell-talepublishing.com.

Thank you for your support of the author's rights.

Published in the United States of America

## *Dedication*

This book is dedicated to all of the men and women throughout the world battling the mental load. With the following tips and techniques, I believe we can work together to make the changes necessary to bring us all relief, peace, and much-needed joy, and to help future generations learn to share the load more equally.

# *INTRODUCTION*

## What is the Mental Load (or Mental Labor)?

I find it rather amusing that I'm starting this book on December 26, 2018. First, it's funny (and absolutely, positively wonderful) that for the next 10 days I will have a MUCH lighter mental load than I carry the rest of the year. Hallelujah. Praise the Lord.

It's also ironic that I bore my heaviest mental load probably in the four to five weeks leading up to this day. I know I certainly wasn't alone. Most of us have way too much going on from about the last couple weeks of November up until and including Christmas Day.

I remember working at my dining room table a month ago and feeling completely and utterly overwhelmed. And tired. Almost exhausted. It's not that I didn't sleep well the night before. Thankfully, even though I'm approaching that fun time of life known as menopause I've been sleeping fine overall.

I wasn't physically exhausted. I was mentally exhausted. Perhaps you'll see why. You may even recognize yourself in this story.

I started out that Tuesday at 6:15 a.m. like normal. My sons, Jonathon and Jacob, are teenagers now and for some reason our local high school has started its day at 7:35 a.m. for decades. Thankfully that's changing next year. But I digress.

With the mantra that "breakfast is the most important meal of the day," I've always gotten up before the boys in order to fix them a good meal. If I didn't, they most likely would eat either nothing or some sugary concoction. Nuh-uh. Not in my household. So my day began with brewing coffee and scrambling eggs.

After I served both boys their breakfast and heard them start to utter more than one syllable to each other, I finished packing their lunches. I learned long ago to pack as much of their lunch as possible the night before - a true sanity saver, as I am not a morning person.

Next came the clickety-clack of toenails on our hardwood floors as our three small dogs - Eli, Loki, and Rex (technically my mom's dog but that's another story) - decided to join the land of the living and go outside. I then fed them along with our two cats.

After that I made my bed, got dressed, and put a load of laundry in the washer, something I do every single morning. Some people may cringe at the thought of doing laundry every day, but it's another sanity saver for me. I can't imagine doing it all in one day week after week.

Soon the kids flew out the door and into their vehicles. I said a little prayer for their safety like I do every morning, then put on makeup and fixed my hair while getting my own breakfast started on the stove. It's rather awesome that our main bathroom is right beside the kitchen. It comes in pretty handy.

After doing a little reading during my ten minutes of breakfast, I put my dishes in our dishwasher and got that puppy started. You may be wondering why I start the dish and clothes washers every morning. I'm fortunate to work as an author and grant consultant from home, a fact that has significantly helped my mental load over

the past 18 months. So I don't have to worry about a potential flood while I am away from the house.

In the warmer months I take our dogs for a quick walk before settling down to work, but we live in Indiana where it's still pretty dang dark at 7:30 in the morning during the winter and, of course, normally freezing. So the walk had to be pushed to lunch time that day.

The first thing I do every weekday before I start my consulting work is check our bank account online. I've handled our family's finances ever since I married my husband John. Heck, I even took over *his* finances when we were dating. John has many strengths, but he will be the first to admit handling money is not one of them.

I prefer to balance our checkbook little by little every day, much like the laundry. If it's a Friday, I'll quickly pay bills thanks to glimpsing at a monthly budget sheet I have set up and our bank's online payment system.

If I have time I'll check my personal email account. I know some people do this now on their phone but I can't handle the constant notifications. I did this task that morning and there was a reminder about Jacob's upcoming choir concert. Along with that email was a message from the choir parent organization president, Samantha, asking if I could post flyers in our downtown to promote it. My first thought was, "How on earth can I do that this time of year?" My second thought was, "I love Samantha, she is swamped, and somehow I will carve out time for this."

I checked my calendar and let her know I had 45 minutes in the late afternoon of the following Monday. That would give me time to have dinner before joining my friends for some hoop dancing that evening - one of my favorite hobbies! My calendar is in Outlook, which I of course had just opened, which officially meant my workday had begun - sort of.

My calendar reminded me about my son Jonathon's upcoming 18th birthday celebration and that I probably should order tickets to the Christmas light display show that was a surprise for John for our 20th anniversary. Yep, our first child was born in early December and John and I were married two years previously on December 19. I'm not sure we planned that very well, but I certainly wouldn't change the outcome.

I threw a reminder on the calendar to wrap Jonathon's birthday presents that coming Saturday along with some Christmas presents. I also noticed that I was going to do the readings at our church service that evening. Just then, Loki nuzzled my leg, and I looked down at her freshly groomed face and was glad she and the other dogs had their quarterly haircut done and out of the way the previous week.

I decided since I hadn't officially started my workday yet that I would go ahead and order tickets online to the light show. I was surprised to discover no time slots were available for the night we had planned, but the night of our anniversary was open. This meant I had to call John immediately to make certain he could get that evening off as he works two or three evenings a week.

Ugh. I HAD to get to work! I finally turned my attention to my emails and sighed after I noticed one of my clients asking if I could join them in person for a meeting. I had literally made a vow the day before to not add another thing on my December calendar. Of course I already had blown that to bits by saying I would help promote the choir concert!

I looked at my grant application deadline schedule, weighed the importance of my attendance, and tactfully turned them down, asking them to please update me afterwards if anything pertained to our grant searches or applications. I knew it was more important for me to stay at home to concentrate on a grant application for them that was due the end of the month.

After wading through the rest of my emails, it was time to put the wet clothes in the dryer. I then grabbed some tea and got to work on an application. I think I was able to work quietly for an entire 50 minutes before my phone rang. It was my mother, who lives in a nearby assisted living facility. She had a question about the doctor she and I were visiting the next morning. Mom also had an addition to her grocery list, which I noted.

Before getting back to work I decided to check on my Christmas list to see how I was doing. Thankfully I start Christmas shopping in early November, but there were still five or six things I needed to order or run out and buy. I marked my calendar for that coming Friday to order a few things online (thank you, God, for Amazon and Amazon Prime) and marked it again to pick up some other final things the following week.

I noticed the upcoming holiday parties John and I were going to attend as well. I silently saluted the amazing, probably exhausted women behind them all. Finally, I turned my attention back to my grant application. But of course, the dryer decided to stop at that moment, so I leapt up to fold and hang clothes so nothing would be wrinkled. I do own an iron and ironing board, but I can't even tell you when I last used them.

My phone rang again and this time it was the water softener salt delivery guy. I told him that I was home and he said he would arrive in 10 minutes. I answered some mails and let him in after corralling the dogs so they wouldn't overwhelm the poor man with their crazy jumping.

I was able to return to my application and work steadily for about 90 minutes with minimal interruptions. My stomach began to growl and I had to force myself to find a good stopping point to have some lunch. Even though I work from home, I try to take at least a half hour lunch break. I unloaded the dishwasher, threw some leftovers in the microwave, and started some rice in the rice cooker for our dinner that evening.

After eating while catching up with the world on Facebook, I took the dogs for a walk. Most of the time I try to meditate as we go, but on that day my brain was in a whirl (I wonder why?) After I got home I decided to quickly put the clothes away before returning to work.

Outlook reminded me that I had a grant professionals meeting the next Tuesday that still required some odds and ends for me to complete. I quickly took care of those and then, to my dismay, I saw an email requesting a meeting during the Thursday evening of the following week. This was for the campaign committee for one of our mayoral candidates. The candidate is awesome and I knew we had a lot of work to do starting in January. It was important for me as the volunteer coordinator to attend. With a sigh I replied yes.

That's when the feeling of complete and utter exhaustion hit me. My neck and shoulders were tight and tense. There were just so many things to remember. Even with the help of Outlook and reminders on my phone, I felt like that joke that's circulated on the Internet about a typical woman's mind. It resembles a computer browser with hundreds of tabs open. All. The. Time.

My story perfectly illustrates the concept of the mental load, or as some call it, mental labor. This is not to be confused with emotional labor.

Arlie Hochschild talked about emotional labor in her 1983 book *The Managed Heart: Commercializations of Human Feeling.* In a November 2018 Atlantic Magazine interview, Hochschild stated [1] "Emotional labor, as I introduced the term in *The Managed Heart*, is the work, for which you're paid, which centrally involves trying to feel the right feeling for the job. This involves evoking and suppressing feelings. Some jobs require a lot of it, some a little of it."

Mental labor, or the mental load, involves the many — and extremely varied — tasks that are involved in managing a household and/or workplace. This topic has exploded over the past couple of years, especially for women. As stated in an October 2017 Washington Post article [2], "The constant stress of trying to stay organized — and to remember to execute so many tasks every single day — is affecting women's relationships with their spouses, children, friends, and colleagues. They are experiencing mental, emotional, and physical fatigue trying to stay on top of it all."

---

1 https://www.theatlantic.com/family/archive/2018/11/arlie-hochschild-housework-isnt-emotional-labor/576637/

2 https://www.washingtonpost.com/lifestyle/home/is-an-uneven-mental-load-creating-tension-in-your-house-here-are-4-ways-to-fix-it/2017/10/16/e7d66bf6-adf2-11e7-a908-a3470754bbb9_story.html?utm_term=.e2bb81ec7424

The following Business Wire graphic summarizes the situation well:

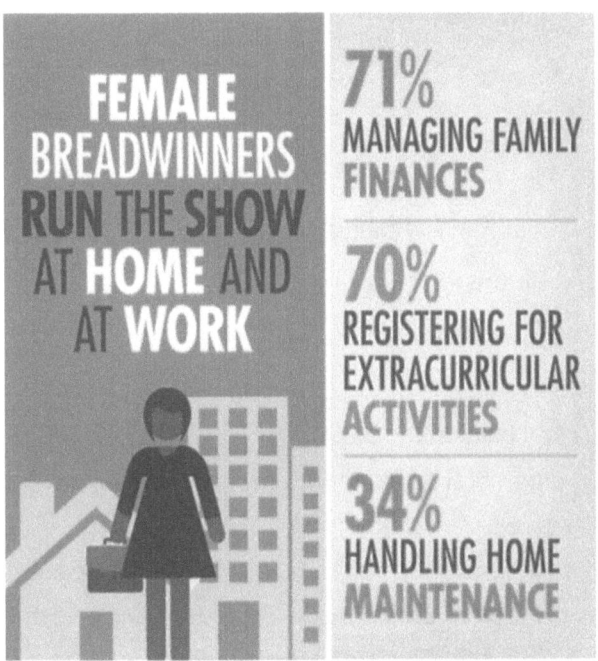

Yes, women carry the mental load most of the time. However, I know some men have it as well. My brother Mark is one of them. I interviewed him recently to get a picture of one of his typical days.

Mark captures all of his "to do's" every morning. He not only works in the insurance industry but also owns his own business called Expo Design. Here's what Mark had on his list for the day in his Florida home when I spoke with him on a recent morning:

- Go through insurance tasks
- Review Expo Design tasks
- Remove bushes
- Take dishes out of dishwasher

- Set up the bedroom for guests
- Prepare for upcoming Tony Robbins course
- Call Matt and review everything for Expo
- Get financials done
- Put up signs in house
- Clean golf cart
- Get in a bike ride
- Call Anthem about medical claims
- Review 401(k) for this year
- Make sure the Schwab account is all set up with new stocks
- Take out the garbage
- Wash sheets and blankets

Suddenly I didn't feel so alone in feeling overwhelmed! Men definitely carry this load as well.

According to a November 2017 report from the US Census, over 16% of households in the United States alone are led by single dads [3]. That's just over 52 million men. I find it hard to believe they don't have some sort of mental load going all the time! And millions of other men around the world are lugging it around, too.

So it's obvious that this book won't just focus on women. It may often highlight women's struggles, but it will recognize the load that *everyone* carries.

This book won't make the mental load completely disappear. Unless you're a hermit living alone in a one room cabin in some woods in the middle of Elk Droppings, Montana, you have to carry at least a little of it. I'm afraid it's just how life goes, Folks.

---

[3] https://www.census.gov/newsroom/press-releases/2017/living-arrangements.html

This book WILL help you lighten the load by at least 50% in the following areas:

- Home
- Marriage/Partnerships
- Children
- Pets
- Transportation
- Career
- Birthdays and celebrations
- Vacations (yes, even these are filled with mental loads)
- Holidays
- Hobbies
- Caring for a parent or other relative
- Volunteering/Church activities

We'll work together to lighten the mental load through technology and other methods. I am literally going on the journey with you as I write this book and I am incredibly excited!

Up until about two years ago, I thought I was doing OK with my mental labor. A friend of mine who doesn't have kids asked me once how I did it all. I simply replied, "I'm really organized!" Yes, I would have the occasional wave hit me of feeling overwhelmed or weary. But most of the time I was able to keep all the balls in the air while I juggled tasks from day to day.

In November 2016, my mom was diagnosed with dementia after yet another fall. My two siblings and I had suspected something was wrong but we weren't able to persuade Mom to get any help. This was the proverbial straw that broke the camel's back and we hurriedly moved her from South Bend, Indiana to an assisted living facility just five minutes from my home near Indianapolis.

The three of us "divided and conquered" her care. My sister Vicky lives in Florida, so she supports everything from a distance and does all she can for Mom when she visits. My brother stepped up and he now handles Mom's finances and insurance along with his wife Janie. I can't express my gratitude enough that I don't have to deal with THAT stuff!

I take care of Mom's day-to-day needs such as groceries, medication purchases, doctor, dentist, and eye appointments, and the general weird emergencies that typically pop up about once a month. I make sure we have some fun as well, of course! Having her here to participate in things like my son's choir concerts is a joy. I feel lucky to still have her on this earth at 86 years of age.

However, I've gradually felt my mental load get heavier as a result of being one of her caregivers. Thus, I've been a bit more, um… cranky. In the past I've not been one to curse too often. My cursing has increased dramatically over the past couple of years!

I'm definitely ready for some changes like millions of others in the world.

Before we start this journey to lighten our mental load, we'll take a look at what got us to this point. How did we become a society with minds like computers with hundreds of tabs open?

We'll also talk about how to prevent adding to other people's mental labor. We'll discuss the steps we must take to prevent carrying too much of a mental load in our retirement years - the period of life that is supposed to be easy and relaxing but is sometimes just as busy as our working years! Finally, we'll talk about how to find time to relax, unwind, and take care of ourselves more often to get a necessary break from that mental labor.

Before we begin, I'd like to thank the French Cartoonist commonly known as Emma for bringing the mental load to the world's attention a couple years ago. When I first saw her comic highlighting this topic I literally read it three times. In fact she published a graphic novel on the mental load at the same time, which I just purchased. It's been such an eye-opener to realize this is a problem facing people not just in the United States, but worldwide. According to the French Institute of Statistics, women are still devoting 25 more hours a week to chores than men. It was almost a relief to see someone finally creating a label for what so many of us deal with every day.

It's like they say, you can't solve a problem unless you properly identify it. Emma's brilliance helped everyone around the globe finally start talking about and working on lessening the mental load.

I'm ready to start this journey with you. Let's dive in!

## *Chapter One*

### How Did We Get Here?

**Where Did This Enormous Mental Load Come From?**

I'll never forget my folklore professor telling us during a class in 1990 at Indiana University about how men and women were actually considered equal a century or more ago in the U.S. A man's role of either working outside of the home or farming was no better than a woman's role of taking care of the home and children. Both were essential for a family to thrive and do well.

I'm not sure how true that was, but the concept sounded great to me. I'm glad, however, that women have more choices today. According to the U.S. Department of Labor, in 1920, 21% of people in the U.S. workforce were women. Today, that number has risen to almost 50%. As more women have entered the workplace, however, various home and parenting responsibilities haven't been shifting accordingly.

Men *are* taking on more hands-on parenting tasks than their fathers before them. I remember my mother marveling at John's parenting skills 18 years ago when our oldest was just a newborn. He had left our table at a restaurant to change Jonathon in the men's restroom.

"Your father never once changed a diaper," she commented. I laughed to myself as I remembered him asking Mom once where the forks were in our house. Dad was a good provider, a loving husband, and a great father. Other than handling our finances, he left the rest of the home and childcare responsibilities to Mom. She didn't work outside the home and did a wonderful job with my siblings and me.

Men have made progress, and my husband and several of our male friends are a great example of this. But research finds that even as more women enter the work force and men take on more chores, there's still a burden many women seem to carry all by ourselves: the mental load.

Why? As my other son Jacob would say, blame society. Women typically adopt this mental labor because our mothers did it and so did our grandmothers. We also worry that the blame for any family or domestic failures will fall squarely on us.

What about same-sex couples raising children today? According to a May 2018 New York Times article [4], research has consistently found that same-sex couples divide up chores more equally. But when gay and lesbian couples have children, they often begin to divide things as heterosexual couples do, according to new data for larger, more representative samples of the gay population. Though the couples are still more equitable, one partner often has higher earnings, and the other one has a greater share of household chores and childcare. The article states that this shows these roles are not just about gender. Work and much of society are still built for single-earner families.

Let's also consider the stay at home dads. My husband performed the latter role for well over 18 months at one time in our marriage.

A man from "across the pond" in the U.K. named John Adams wrote that the mental load is real and it's not just borne by women. He stated in a June 2017 article in The Telegraph [5] "I'm a man. I am the main caregiver for my kids and have been since 2011. It's my wife who fulfills the traditional role of breadwinner while I do the majority of the childcare and run the household (by my own admission, with varying degrees of success)."

"Regardless of gender, we all feel a Mental Load," Adams continued. "The burdens may differ, but we're all under pressure and we need to

---

4 https://www.nytimes.com/2018/05/16/upshot/same-sex-couples-divide-chores-much-more-evenly-until-they-become-parents.html

5 https://www.telegraph.co.uk/family/parenting/mental-load-real-feminists-wrong-think-women-feel/

explain it, understand it and deal with it. There is an unseen, unrecognized, unfair mental burden involved in running a household."

I mentioned single dads in the introduction, but any single parent has certainly got to be performing a great deal of mental labor. A therapist I saw online called it the "extra plus sized mental load." To all the single parents out there, I desperately hope you get some great tips and help from this book. I admire you more than I can adequately express in this publication.

Working dads certainly have their share of a mental load. I see it with my own husband who sometimes works 60+ hours a week. One of our dear friends, Gary, travels for work at least two or three weeks every month and is often away from his wife and daughters.

Josh Levs, a leading American expert on working dads and the author of a book called *All In,* said men's invisible load has to do with mental health and stress [6]. "It's not that men have more mental health problems than women," Levs said. "But men are less open than women about mental health issues. Men are more likely to keep anxieties, stresses, and depression problems to themselves and they are less likely than women to seek out support for those problems."

To summarize, both women and men often experience this crushing mental load. How on earth did it get so bad in recent decades that we are losing sleep and becoming more anxious and depressed?

One reason is the massive size of some of our houses. In the past 40 years the average size of the American home has increased by about 1,000 feet. In Australia, the average house size has more than doubled in the past 60 years. Bigger houses = more upkeep, more to clean, more to repair, and more to keep track of. That can be a job in itself. In fact, our friend Rick has a part-time job taking care of a mansion owned by a successful local orthodontist!

---

[6] https://thingsdadsdo.wordpress.com/2017/06/20/do-fathers-have-an-invisible-load-too/

Owning a car, let alone two or more, definitely adds to the mental load. Until World War II and into the late 1940s, many Americans did not own a car. In 2001, the average licensed driver owned 1.1 vehicles. Keeping track of the repairs, maintenance, cleaning, and fueling for one vehicle is challenging enough. Obviously the more vehicles you add, the more mental labor involved.

As we discussed earlier, it's common for both partners in a relationship to have jobs these days. Yes, they are often splitting chores a little more evenly than years ago, but the *management* of all those tasks unfortunately falls to one person most of the time. Even if you don't have children, it's tiring.

A friend of mine once called her mental labor "my second shift." She and her husband don't have kids, but they work full-time outside the home, have a dog, and own two cars. They also have elderly parents battling health issues. My friend works from 8-4:30 Monday through Friday, then starts her "second shift" at 5 when she gets home, as her husband is an attorney who often has evening meetings.

The mental load goes to a whole new level when you add children to the mix. Birth rates are falling around the world, so you would think that having smaller families would help with the mental labor many of us take on when raising children. However, even having just one child creates a big mental load. Today in the U.S., children have homework starting in *kindergarten*! A friend of mine has middle school daughters who are sometimes up past 10 o'clock at night working on homework and they often need help from a parent. As of this writing, I am 48 years old. I didn't have homework until I was in fifth grade, and it took me maybe half an hour to complete it.

Parents are expected to be at their children's schools more often. I remember my mother, who was a stay at home mom, chaperoning two of my field trips. That's it. I didn't feel deprived or neglected either. Now most parents face the pressure to become active members of their PTO or other school-based organization.

Kids are involved in more extracurricular activities than they were just a few decades ago. Author KJ Dell'Antonia tackled this subject in her book *How to Be a Happier Parent*.

CNN shared some highlights from Dell'Antonia in August 2018 [7]. Unsupervised and unstructured playtime has decreased for all children since 1981. Parents spend more time driving children to and from activities and organizing and attending them than they have in previous generations. Twenty-seven percent of all trips taken in 2012 were for the sole purpose of attending an organized sporting event. And 35% of parents, according to a single survey, say that managing their child's school and extracurricular transportation arrangements is more stressful than taxes!

How about our pets? They bring joy to so many of us. According to a survey by the American Pet Products Association (APPA) [8], 68 percent of American households own a pet. Pets now have a place in nearly 85 million American homes -- just over five million more than in 2015.

I used to dream about having many pets as a child, much like my sister. I've been an animal lover for as long as I can remember. Growing up I remember my sister's family at one time or another owning a dog, cat, guinea pig, lizard, hamsters, fish, and/or other creatures. Now that I'm married with kids, we've often been called the Thornton Animal Shelter. Our list of various pets through the years is similar to what my sister and her family had. We now have three dogs and two cats. For the most part, they do bring us joy. For example, I love my daily walks with the dogs.

But, of course, cats and dogs add to the mental load. At the very minimum you have their watering, feeding, grooming, flea and heartworm prevention medication, and veterinarian schedules to keep track of. Dogs need to be walked, especially if you live in an apartment or you have larger

---

7 https://www.cnn.com/2018/08/29/health/extracurriculars-happiness-parenting-strauss/index.html

8 https://www.americanpetproducts.org/press_industrytrends.asp

breeds. Some pets are fine for you to leave alone over a weekend, but that doesn't work with canines. So you can add boarding schedules whenever you need to take a weekend or longer trip.

And if something goes wrong with one of them? Like with a child, it causes major stress. Right now we're looking for a new home for one of our cats, as she has had litter box issues for the past two years. We have tried *everything* to fix the problem. Finding someone who has a barn who would like an older declawed cat is not easy. I know eventually something will work out. While I will miss Princess, the relief of not having to constantly worry about whether or not she is going to ruin our (almost) new carpet will be great.

As if the mental labor isn't big enough with just running a home and family, some of us carry our jobs into the mix. As I mentioned in my other book, *Joy to You and Me (At Work!),* the average workweek has risen from 40 to 46-47 hours per week. Thanks to advances in technology, a lot of folks don't stop working once they leave the office. Or, if they're like me, their office is in their home. It's easy for those work/home boundaries to get blurry or be eliminated altogether.

Even during those "true" work hours, many people carry a mental load. But wait, that's what we're getting paid to do, right? In this case it's defined as work that goes on every day that you don't get paid for. I call it "other duties as assigned" that aren't in most job descriptions. They may include tasks such as purchasing cards and making sure they're signed by everyone, buying snacks, planning events, getting the coffee, buying birthday cakes, cleaning up after meetings, and taking notes.

I actually used to love doing many of those things when I worked in the typical office setting. But not everyone is like me. If you don't have a good system in place, these tasks can be quite draining.

Speaking of cards and events, celebrations require mental labor. Of course we want to plan and execute these events for the people we love. My son Jonathon will graduate high school in May and I've already picked out the location for his party and a tentative date, which I intend to confirm by mid-January. Even with keeping things simple by serving hors d'oeuvres, beverages, and of course, a fabulous cake, I know my mental load will be heavier in the coming months. I've already been thinking of what mementos and photos will be on display that afternoon. It's going to be fun and I'm excited for my son, but I realize once it's over I will be pretty dang tired unless I implement ideas from this book!

Then we have holidays, another category of celebrations. This is where I think the mental load often goes into overdrive. I know women who stay up until 2 o'clock in the morning getting ready to host Christmas parties. A good friend of mine takes three days to unload and put up her Christmas decorations - and these are just indoor ones. The Christmas card process for some folks no longer involves simply buying boxes of cards from the store, then signing, addressing, and mailing them. Now a lot of us schedule a photo session with a professional photographer to get the perfect family photo, look through every proof to find the best picture, and finally design a card online.

I remember my mother baking maybe three or four types of Christmas cookies every year. And keep in mind she was a stay at home mom. Now I see people making six or more kinds of cookies. I know a lot of people love baking, me included, but others don't like it very much. But they still feel the pressure of the season to bake like crazy and work to have a Christmas like what you see in magazines.

Not everyone celebrates Christmas of course, but there are other holidays that can create just as much pressure. Halloween decorations used to involve some carved jack-o'-lanterns and maybe a cute spooky candy dish or two. Now you can't walk into any big box hardware store in August without seeing aisles and aisles of indoor and outdoor decorations. These range from two inches high to 10 feet tall and go from cute to downright scary or horrible. Some people in my neighborhood put out so many decorations starting in late September that you can barely see their grass or landscaping.

When I was a child, poking some holes in an old sheet worked great to create a ghost costume. If you had anything more elaborate than that, you often wore that costume two, three, or four more times in future years. And it wasn't a big deal because that's what everybody else did. Now, however, things are more complicated. Do you go to the party store and buy a costume or order one online? Do you know anyone that actually sews these days that can make you or your child something unique? How can you give your child a totally different, better costume than last year?

I could go on and on, since we have so many holidays, but you get the point. Thanks to the pressure from Pinterest, various magazines, numerous home and garden television shows, and our own neighbors, many times holiday celebrations have gone from the enjoyment of simple pleasures to working to plan over-the-top affairs that involve a lot more time, creativity, and money. Don't get me wrong, I know some people love to go all out each season and it makes them very happy. But others feel like they *have* to do it all whether they like it or not.

Surely we can escape the mental load when we go on vacation, right? Or through our hobbies - if we are able to have those with all that is going on in life. Yes and no. Planning a vacation where you go away from home can take weeks of preparation, if not months. You have to focus on transportation first. If you're going by plane, train, or boat, you have to check prices often to book a fare that's not an arm and a leg. If you travel by car, it's important to get it checked over to make certain the tires and other components can safely handle the distance.

If you are traveling with others, you have to communicate with them to go over schedules to pick potential dates that work for everyone. Once the dates and transportation are all settled, then you have to figure out who will take care of your home while you're away. Do you need a house sitter? Or can your next-door neighbor simply check on things for you every couple of days?

Then it's time to budget your money accordingly and start your packing list. You'll probably need to get items from the store or online such as sunscreen, toiletries, and maybe even a new bathing suit. Or maybe you're going somewhere cold - not MY idea of a fun vacation but I know a lot of people love it - and you need long underwear, ski boots, etc.

If you have small children, you may need to get all the necessary gear ready such as a pack and play, traveling highchair, a "potty" seat, and so much more. Not to mention tons of diapers, wipes, blankets, burp cloths, extra clothes in case of blowout situations, and anything else you typically carry in a diaper bag.

Don't forget everything you have to do beforehand at work to make certain the world will still keep turning while you are away.

After you're packed, ready to go, and finally on your way to a great time, that mental load still lingers on occasion. One of my girlfriends confessed to me once that it takes a good two to three days for her to finally stop thinking about work whenever she travels for a vacation. And this is someone who actually does not check her work email or voicemail when she is out of the office!

Unfortunately, once we return from vacation, it can be way too easy for that mental labor to come crashing right back down on top of us. Unpacking and catching up on laundry, piles of mail and work can make us wonder if going on vacation was worth it in the first place.

I love my hobbies and they are also terrific for escaping the mental load. But some of them require some planning and mental labor as well. I enjoy walking a half marathon now every spring. Of course this requires preparation. I have to schedule three training walks each week on my calendar 14 weeks ahead of time to make certain my body will be ready for 13.1 miles. I have to buy a new pair of shoes and check to see if other attire may need to be replaced.

I also enjoy hoop dancing, which is essentially dancing with a hula-hoop. I do this hobby either alone or with others. Once a week I hoop dance with other people, which requires scheduling time to meet up in a park or working with a local venue so we can dance indoors during the colder months. Most of the time I can post all of this on social media, however, not everyone is on it and I have to text certain people.

And how about the millions of people who can't take vacations or enjoy hobbies? I'm talking about all of the caregivers out there taking care of elderly parents, special needs children, or spouses with poor health. Unless you've been living under a rock, you know that the mental labor for these folks is stressful. It's often rewarding and wonderful, and I personally wouldn't have it any other way with my mom. But it sometimes makes my head spin. I know there are a lot of other men and women in my shoes.

Women, however, provide the majority of informal care to spouses, parents, parents-in-law, friends, and neighbors. They play many roles while caregiving—hands-on health provider, care manager, friend, companion, surrogate decision-maker and advocate [9]. I've seen men play this role as well, including both of my brothers-in-law who did such an amazing job of caring for their parents during the last few years of their lives.

I am fortunate that Mom can afford to live in a nice assisted living facility just five minutes from my home. I'm just one of the many "team" members that provide care for her. I know there are millions of individuals who have no choice but to be caregivers on a 24/7 basis. It is a beautiful role, but it can also take its toll on a person. According to an AARP Public Policy Institute poll, 35 percent of family caregivers view their health as fair to poor [10].

---

[9] Navaie-Waliser, M., Feldman, P. H., Gould, D. A., Levine, C. L., Kuerbis A. N., & Donelan, K. (2002). When the caregiver needs care: The plight of vulnerable caregivers. *American Journal of Public Health 92(3)*, 409-413

[10] https://www.elitedaily.com/life/stress-of-a-caregiver/1065227

Finally, let's look at another way we help others and the mental labor involved - volunteering. I firmly believe giving back to your community and beyond is vital. I've served my community in various ways ever since I was in high school, and my kids have been raised to do the same. We've volunteered together through Scouting, church, and non-profit organization activities.

Signing up for projects and showing up to implement them doesn't require much of a mental load. Most of the time the work is fun, beneficial to others, and good for the soul. Without "worker bees", tasks simply wouldn't be accomplished. It's valuable service. This is what I currently do for my church. I deliver meals every few months for our Monthly Graced Meals program and I often give readings up at the front of church during mass.

When you move over to the more complicated roles such as serving on a board of directors or a committee, then you're entering the realm of the mental load. I am a proud member of the Noblesville Main Street board of directors and chair of the organization's design committee. As I mentioned earlier, I also serve on the committee for one of the individuals running for mayor in my city. Finally, I am Vice President of Programming for my local chapter of the Grant Professionals Association. I'm able to serve in these capacities now thanks to my sons being older and my flexible work schedule.

Right now these roles work for me and I love them, but they also add to my mental labor. I have to think through and plan the Main Street design committee agenda every month and, of course, lead the meetings. On the board of directors, I am the "go to gal" for anything grant related. While I do not write the applications, I am responsible for guiding the director to be successful in these efforts.

As Vice President of Programming for my grant professionals group, I'm in charge of finding speakers and working with the board to plan the dates, times, meals, and locations of monthly meetings. I definitely have help and don't do everything alone. This is the strongest local board I've ever seen and we often have a lot of fun.

Last but not least, I am the volunteer coordinator for the previously mentioned election committee. This position made sense for me, since I did similar work when I was employed with the City of Noblesville, Indiana. We are using one of the many online volunteer management systems available to make the process as seamless as possible. However, I definitely perform mental labor in this role.

Why do I serve in these high-level volunteer positions? I don't have to. I could stick to the one-off projects that give me a great deal of satisfaction and still help others. But I'm a firm believer that I should use the talents that the Lord gave me. The high-level roles are a great fit for my skills.

To summarize all these areas of life that have created our current mental load, the reason so many of us deal with a huge one can be summed up in one simple word. MORE.

More square feet in our homes, more vehicles, more than one job supporting a family. More kids' activities, more pets, and more invisible responsibilities at work and increased hours spent on the job. More elaborate holidays and celebrations. More complicated vacations and hobbies. More caregiving responsibilities, especially as we get older, and more ways to help our community.

After reading this chapter, I'm sure you're ready to scream, chuck it all, and move to the place in Montana that I mentioned in the introduction. Sorry, but there is no such town called Elk Droppings, Montana. Apparently there is a product called Montana Elk Droppings, which are chocolate covered almonds. But let's get back to our subject.

I didn't write this chapter to bring you down, but rather to help you see the extent of the problem and its origins. I promise you there is hope and we can make some big changes. We obviously can't and shouldn't get rid of all of our responsibilities. But some of them are optional, and we'll explore how to gradually (or suddenly) let go of these things in our lives without our world collapsing.

We'll talk about the many ways we can lighten our mental loads by 50 to 75% in each of the areas I mentioned. We'll explore various techniques that have worked for others as well as some fabulous free or low cost technology.

Hopefully in 10 to 20 years all of the depressing information I shared earlier will be ancient history, something we can look back on and sigh with relief knowing we've made the right changes and won't repeat those mistakes. I believe lightening this mental load will make us a happier, healthier, more productive society.

And as the saying goes, it all starts at home.

# *Chapter Two*

## Home Sweet Home

### The Mental Labor of Home Ownership

Most of us start our post high school, college, or military lives by renting an apartment, condominium, or house. Although the home ownership rate in the United States has declined somewhat recently compared to other countries in the developed world, it's still a big dream for many Americans to eventually stop renting and buy a house as soon as possible.

"Despite home buying being a long and often exhausting process, and homeownership being a time-consuming and frankly expensive venture, 75 percent of Americans say it's a priority, according to NerdWallet's 2018 Home Buyer Report,"[11] Nerd Wallet expert Tim Manni said. "If recessions, high prices, and stress can't kill the American dream, I'm not sure anything will. The American desire to own a home is incredibly resilient."

There are many reasons why owning a home is a great idea, and, of course, reasons why it's not so great. We won't get into both sides of the fence in this book, but we will talk about a few facets of home ownership and how to relieve the mental labor with each.

### Finances

Managing your finances well is important for home ownership and just about everything else in life. For example, my sons are both still in high school and work part time jobs. We've taught them how to create and

---

[11] https://themreport.com/daily-dose/04-25-2018/the-declining-stress-of-homeownership

monitor a monthly budget and how their checking and savings accounts work. Both Jonathon and Jacob saved up to buy their first cars. They pay for oil changes, car insurance, and fuel. And of course they take care of their own entertainment and some of their clothing expenses. Right now things aren't too complicated for them.

I know all of that will change later on when they are independent young adults renting their first place. Their future will include, at a minimum, rent, phone, and some utility payments in addition to their vehicle expenses. We're hoping to avoid student loans altogether or to at least keep them to a minimum. Both boys will start out at nearby colleges, work part-time throughout their college career, and take advantage of scholarship opportunities. Jonathon has already won one scholarship that will be a big help in paying for college.

Creating some kind of system for handling finances even before you own a home will definitely help prevent what can be a crushing mental load in life. Not only does it make bill paying easier, but it also helps you manage your money intelligently so you can build wealth.

Oh how I wish I could go back in time and tell all of this to my "post college self!" I had to learn things the hard way later on in life - and I'm still learning. But I'm doing better.

Let's first look at some ways you can learn to be wise with your money. Trust me, if you don't have this skill, your overall mental load will be twice as bad (and I am talking from experience here!). If you already have this wisdom and have done a great job managing and building your wealth, feel free to skip ahead a few paragraphs. If you don't have this knowledge and need some assistance, I know of some fantastic resources to help you.

My favorite expert on this topic is Dave Ramsey, an American personal finance guru, businessman, and author. Mr. Ramsey has helped millions of people turn their financial lives around. What I like about him is that he made mistakes, learned from them, and eventually built his wealth the smart way. He even went through the pain of bankruptcy before turning his life around.

Mr. Ramsey offers numerous resources on his website, daveramsey.com, ranging from free downloads, apps, guides, calculators, and forms to books and his Financial Peace University course offered at hundreds of locations across the United States or online. The books and course are quite reasonable.

Suze Orman is another bestselling author on personal finance, with over 25 million books in circulation, available in 12 languages worldwide. In addition to her television show, she offers a variety of resources on her website, suzeorman.com. The homepage offers a Choose Your Goal section with topics such as credit and debit, saving, investing, home ownership, student loans, retirement, life insurance, family and estate planning, and Social Security.

Another route I'm going to encourage my sons to follow is to take a personal finance course at our local community college, Ivy Tech. Here's a recent class description:

"This course will prepare you for a lifetime of worthwhile personal financial planning. The tools you will learn are useful, realistic, and easy to work into your regular routine. They will help you gain control over the financial impact of the choices you make. You'll learn to create and use a budget, borrow and invest wisely, make intelligent decisions about insurance, and plan for your financial future. You'll develop a retirement savings plan, and you'll be better prepared to make large purchases and plan for taxes. You'll learn the essentials of household bookkeeping, record-keeping requirements, and much, much more."

This course is currently offered here in Indiana for about $130. I know similar classes are held all over the U.S. I don't think you can find a better investment for such an important topic to help you live a happier life without the load of financial difficulties weighing you down.

Now that you have some guidance on how to be smart with money, let's lighten the labor of managing it. I love how technology can help us with our finances. I've been a big fan of Quicken software for decades now. It's available in different languages, offers free mobile apps, and helps you not only pay bills and people, but track these expenses. I like its online bill-paying feature. Quicken makes balancing a checkbook and your budget fast and easy. As of this writing, plans start at $35 a year.

Of course there are other online or computer based systems you can use to help with home finances. The Balance recommends Quicken for an overall system but also suggests Mint for budgeting and expense tracking, YNAB to help you improve your financial literacy and manage your monthly budget, Mvelopes for zero based budgeting, and TurboTax for - what else - taxes [12].

Speaking of taxes - they can be a mental load all by themselves. I can't imagine doing ours anymore without some sort of software or hiring an accountant. But even with this help, you can still be bogged down if you don't have an organized system for gathering necessities throughout the year for tax preparation. Whether you scan everything and keep electronic copies of receipts, are more like me and still like to keep paper copies, or a combination of both, putting everything consistently in one place throughout the year will help make tax time easier and prevent a lot of mental labor.

Going back to daily or weekly financial tasks, what if you're just not ready or willing to utilize technology for all of your budgeting and bill paying tasks? At the very least, I would encourage you to pay your bills online either through the provider or your bank's online bill payment system. Just be careful with the former because sometimes they charge convenience fees.

I pay all my bills online through my bank and it is a Godsend. It's great to set up different payee addresses just one time and create automatic payments for those bills with amounts that don't change from month-to-month. You can even pay people through this system. And many banks also allow you to deposit checks by simply taking a photo of them.

---

[12] https://www.thebalance.com/best-personal-finance-software-4171938

I like being able to view transactions on my computer each day and to easily transfer money between accounts by tapping just a few keys. I've caught some unauthorized transactions in the past by keeping an eye on my account this way, which obviously saves a lot of headaches and aggravation.

Of course, when doing any sort of financial transactions online, you need to take precautions to make certain you have a secure connection. I never do any bill paying or viewing of my bank account when I am away from home. Even when I am taking care of banking online in my dining room, I make certain to quickly log out when I am finished.

Watch out for the email scam when you receive a message that looks like it's from your bank. If it truly appears that you have an email from your bank, log on to that institution's site and get your message there.

Taking care of our family's banking and bill payments online saves me at least an hour a week if not more. I remember sitting down every week or every other week decades ago and writing out checks/envelopes and "licking and sticking" multiple stamps. I had to carve out 45 minutes or more for the process. Then there was the hour or so each month of getting a hard copy of our bank statement and balancing our checkbook.

Now I just look at our monthly budget, which is a simple Word document that breaks down our income and what is typically due on what week of the month, and pay that week's bills every Friday online through our bank. I keep any paper copies of bills all together in a file in order by due date and do the same for any email bills on my computer. The rest is taken care of by automated bill payment or withdrawal from our account. I also take a minute at the start of every weekday to check our account online and do some quick balancing.

Being smart with your finances and getting organized in managing them is an important first step in reducing the mental labor of taking care of your home. By using some or all of these tips, you can decrease your financial mental load by up to 75%.

**Home Repair/Maintenance/Upkeep**

This section could be a book in and of itself. You could take some drastic measures to help reduce the mental labor of home ownership by buying or downsizing to a smaller home. You could also live in a condominium where you pay for someone else to handle all outdoor upkeep and maintenance. The tiny home trend is exploding thanks to its appeal of reducing the physical and mental labor of home ownership and environmental impact. If you do choose one of these options, you'll drastically reduce your mental load with homeownership. But they may not be viable for a lot of people.

Repairing, maintaining, and taking care of a home involves a multitude of monthly, seasonal, and yearly tasks. Most of these you can do yourself, but some involve paying a professional. For this mental load, and many others we will talk about later on in this book, I highly recommend a checklist.

I adore checklists. I use them in my grant consulting business to help break down the many components of large applications. Turns out they're useful in both business and in the home. The site lifeoptimizer.org (how's that for a great name that relates to what we're talking about?) says the reason why checklists are good is simple - without them, it's easy for us to forget things [13]. Don't we know that too well when we refer to mental labor?

The site goes on to say that besides helping you do your task correctly every time, other benefits of using a checklist include:

1. Saving your brainpower for more creative things. Since you don't have to remember all the steps you need to take, you can use your brainpower for something more creative. That's one goal we can reach after reducing the mental load!

---

[13] https://www.lifeoptimizer.org/2011/03/10/using-checklists/l

2. Saving time. You eliminate having to remember the steps, so you can devote the entire time on doing the task. Hallelujah! Less crap to keep track of.
3. You can delegate more easily. If you ever want to delegate a task, your checklist will make it easier for you to hand it over. Delegation is another wonderful tool we will refer to often. By giving the checklist to the person you delegate to, you can describe exactly what you want.

I found numerous checklists available online to help you keep track of your monthly, seasonal, and yearly home maintenance tasks. The site prudentreviews.com, which was created specifically to help make life easier for homeowners, offers an excellent one [14]. Once you have your checklist, I recommend automating as many tasks as possible.

My furnace and air-conditioning maintenance man, Ryan, sends us a postcard every fall and spring as a reminder to schedule our yearly furnace and air conditioner tune up. I receive an email reminder every year when it's time to tune our piano. For companies that don't send notices, I like to schedule an automatic yearly reminder in Outlook for other maintenance tasks.

Can you afford to eliminate some of these tasks altogether? My husband John works for a company that sells and installs a variety of products for the home, including windows, doors, siding, insulation, garage floor coverings, and gutter systems. We finally purchased the covered gutters, or rainwater management system as they fondly call it, two years ago. It's been a huge relief not to have to worry about cleaning our gutters ever again! And they're guaranteed for life, so we know we've made a good investment.

You don't have to spend thousands of dollars, however, to bring some relief in this area. Do you have any teenagers in your neighborhood that

---

14 https://prudentreviews.com/wp-content/uploads/2018/07/Home-Maintenance-Checklist-Printable.pdf

might be willing to do some outside chores for a little cash? Maybe they can rake leaves for you every fall or help with your spring-cleaning.

Perhaps this is also the time to use the wonderful concept I mentioned a few paragraphs back that is (mostly!) free - delegation. If you have older children, they can pitch in and take care of tasks like checking the smoke detectors, washing windows, and putting down mulch. If you are married or have a partner, this area might be a great opportunity to sit down with the other person to see what tasks can be done together or what they may not mind taking over.

With a good checklist in hand, a little outsourcing, and some delegation, you can cut the mental labor involved with the upkeep, maintenance, and repair of your home by at least half.

**Housecleaning/Housework**

When people talk about the mental load, house cleaning/housework is probably one of the most controversial topics. In fact, from what I've seen, this subject rises to the top of most mental labor discussions. I admit - I have not done well in the past on relieving my own mental load in this area. But things are changing in my household and I hope to help you do the same!

If there's room in your budget, you can help bring relief by hiring someone to clean your home. I realize this isn't for everyone, and for many there's still the stigma that you have to be rich or lazy to pick this option. Believe me, I am neither one of these, and I hired a friend's business long ago to come and clean my home once a month. I'll tell you the reasons why.

1. It frees up my time to volunteer in my community and to help with my sons' activities. It's wonderful to spend those five to six hours a month volunteering at a Noblesville Main Street event, a choir fundraiser, or at a campaign party versus deep cleaning my house. I wasn't able to volunteer as easily when I had to clean our house every two or three weeks.

2. My friend's business does a better job than me! I still do a spring-cleaning every year where I literally tear apart the house and put it back together. I vacuum or wipe down every crack and crevice; de-clutter like mad; organize every drawer and closet; clean blinds, curtains, and windows; and donate at least a minivan full of items to local thrift stores. But no one gets my kitchen or bathrooms cleaner than the ladies who work for Christy. In fact, when I go to deep clean something in the spring, I'm often surprised to see it's already done thanks to their thorough actions.

3. It feels good to help the local economy. When I heard Christy was starting her business three or four years ago, I figured this was a great opportunity to get some reliable help for housecleaning. I have referred her to numerous people who have been thrilled with her services. I love to help others succeed, and I figure in this situation it's a win-win!

4. The house doesn't fall apart when I get sick. I don't get sick very often anymore, but I remember what used to happen before we had a house cleaner and I became ill. I think it took me a whole weekend to get the house back to normal after battling the flu eight years ago. Just thinking of that makes me shudder.

5. It's just a huge freaking relief for anyone who works full-time. To come home after some back-to-back meetings on a "Cleaning Wednesday", as I call it, and look around at my nice, neat, tidy house is almost euphoric. I swear I hear angels singing. It's awesome to realize that I didn't have to give up a Saturday or stay up late on a Friday evening to clean.

Paying someone to clean your home may not be as costly as you think. If you go out to eat a little less often or give up some material goods, you may be able to create some room in your budget. And it's worth it. According to research from Ashley Whillans, assistant professor at Harvard Business

School, people who spend money to save time are happier than those who spend it on material goods - significantly happier [15].

Even with cutting out certain things in our budget, we certainly haven't always been able to afford this option. When my sons were little, I would occasionally hire a "mother's helper" - a teenage girl from our neighborhood who would spend three or four hours entertaining Jonathon and Jacob while I cleaned. Since I was still at home, technically it wasn't babysitting, so it wasn't as expensive as a night out. And the kids enjoyed someone new to play with.

Christy's wonderful service is a huge help nowadays, however, there's still plenty of cleaning left. There's always the picking up and straightening that I need to do the night before her magical cleaning fairies arrive. My husband laughs and calls it the "cleaning before the cleaning." But, to put it simply, housecleaners can't do an effective job for you if they can't reach what needs to be cleaned.

Of course, I do small touch up cleaning jobs between sessions such as scrubbing toilets and wiping down the kitchen sink, stove, and counters. And there's no escaping the everyday jobs like laundry, dishes, etc.

Some people can't afford or simply won't pay someone to clean or help clean their house. I'm sure some of you are shaking your head thinking about my situation wondering why I haven't asked my husband and kids to pitch in. The crazy answer is, years ago I never even thought about it. It goes back to what I discussed in the previous chapter. My mother managed and implemented almost all of the household tasks. I know her mother did the same thing, as my grandpa both worked on his farm and ran a barbershop in downtown South Bend, Indiana.

So when I first married John, I just automatically filled that same role. And even with working a full-time job outside the home at the time, I think I

---

[15] https://www.nbcnews.com/better/health/how-hiring-house-cleaner-made-me-happier-healthier-more-productive-ncna810236

handled things fairly well. I'm a pretty organized, energetic person, which helps. When the boys came along, I was fortunate to find a part-time job working from home for a local nonprofit. John worked a lot of hours at the time, including evenings and weekends, so it just made sense for me to continue to be in charge of the home front.

I did have a light bulb moment when the kids reached kindergarten and first grade. I read an article in a magazine talking about how you could teach your toddlers and preschoolers to always put away one toy before getting out another one. Unfortunately my kids were past that stage at the time, but I remember thinking it was a brilliant concept.

Don't get me wrong. I did start to give the boys some simple chores back then. And when I found a full-time job at City Hall and John became a stay at home dad for 18 months around this time, he had them doing even more chores such as feeding our pets, putting away their own laundry, and helping him with yard work. But when John went back to work full-time, most of the mental labor for housecleaning and other duties fell back on me.

But it doesn't have to be that way and lately I've been realizing it *shouldn't* be that way. And a lot of people are with me! So how do we lighten the burden of the mental labor of housecleaning, which typically falls on one person, without paying somebody?

Of all the articles I've read on this subject, I was impressed to find one written by a man who truly "gets it!" Nick Douglas wrote an article in May 2017 on lifehacker.com entitled *How to Share the Mental Load of Chores With Your Partner.*

Douglas wrote that among straight couples even when men do equal work carrying out household chores, women still disproportionally bear the mental load of keeping track of those chores[16]. This creates a kind of continuous partial attention that takes up energy and raises stress. It also

---

16 https://lifehacker.com/how-to-share-the-mental-load-of-chores-with-your-part-1795657878

forms an invisible hierarchy where men feel like employees running afoul of the boss.

Boom! Mr. Douglas, you nailed it.

He went on to say that men often fail to appreciate or share this invisible management job. "If you can help carry the load, you can relieve your partner's stress and feel less like an underling," he wrote. Douglas went on to share tips on how to do just that.

The first thing a partner can do is *anticipate needs.*

"Don't just do the laundry," Douglas said, "Monitor the hamper and take the initiative to run a load. Examine when your tasks usually need to be done, and plan ahead for them."

The second step is to *write things down.* Nowadays you don't even need a pen and paper for this. Many people have smart phones where they can just set numerous reminders and they are off and running!

The third step is to *automate things.*

"Turn your phone into your manager and eliminate the mental load altogether. Add alarms to those calendar events. Set location-based notifications that remind you, when you're passing the drugstore, to stop in. Move regular shopping trips onto Amazon Subscribe & Save," Douglas advised.

He also says that you need to *learn the skills* for what you don't do so you can serve as a backup when your partner is ill or traveling. For example, if you don't typically do laundry, have your partner show you the basics such as sorting colors, different washer and dryer cycles and their purposes, etc. Speaking of cleaning clothes, I haven't been to the dry cleaners in years thanks to those wonderful kits for the dryer! I've used Dryel and Woolite and have had success with both for clothes I used to have to take to the dry cleaner. These kits save me time and are a relief for my mental load!

Douglas suggested holding family meetings on Sundays to keep everyone apprised of what responsibilities each person has for the coming week and to discuss potentially swapping tasks if needed. And speaking of family, he dedicated a whole paragraph to putting kids to work, saying you can hand off some of the mental load by teaching them to self-manage.

He went on to share that Lifehacker writer Beth Skwarecki asks her kids to "be the boss of cleaning the table," telling her what to pick up while she does all the work. "They love their little power trip but I love that they're actually paying attention to what the mess is and how to clean it." This management-only outsourcing even helps kids learn how to cook before they're old enough to do dangerous tasks themselves.

All of these techniques are especially important when major life changes hit such as an illness or injury, a new job, or having a child. "The more flexible you are with your partner, and the more chores you both feel comfortable swapping, the more you can handle in a crisis," Douglas concluded.

If I ever meet this man, I'm going to give him a huge round of applause. Or a massive hug.

Take a look at the stage of life you're in and think about how the mental load can be shared more in the housecleaning arena. If you're about to get married or to move in with a partner, have a meeting to discuss who will be in charge of implementing AND managing tasks. Once your partner takes over a responsibility, DO NOT think about it anymore. Let them do it *their way* as well. This is tough for me because I sort of have some, shall we say, control freak tendencies. But I'm learning it's worth it to let things go.

I've seen an example of how beautifully this works with one couple we know. We get together once a month with a group of friends for a home cooked meal and board games, rotating the location to someplace new each time. It's an event John and I look forward to and enjoy tremendously.

Whenever we go to our friend Elaine and Dan's house, we see the same efficient routine. Elaine always cooks a fabulous dinner, and once we all enjoy it, Dan steps in to clean up and take care of the dishes. You can tell it's automatic for them and that they've done it for years.

If you're planning on having a family or you've just had a baby, start writing down your child's future chores! I love the chore chart concept because it's essentially another checklist. You can find various chore charts online, and I've seen dozens on smarterparenting.com. With these charts, your kids will soon take charge of their own chores.

As I learned a little late, small children can actually be a big help. Four and five-year-olds can make their beds, set and clear the table, empty the dishwasher, move the laundry from the washer to the dryer and then later fold and put clothes away, vacuum, clean up their toys, and empty small trash cans. All of this requires that you show them how to do everything (which might take a time or two), hold on to your patience, praise them, and give up expectations of perfection.

Older children and teenagers can obviously do more. This is currently my stage in life. I realize that things can be tricky, however, when you factor in school activities and part time jobs. Both of my sons attend high school and work 15-20 hours a week at nearby restaurants. Jacob is involved in jazz band and choir. Naturally we want to make certain they have time to complete their homework.

My sons mow the lawn and help with various outdoor chores in warmer weather. Jonathon is in charge of taking out trash and recycling and he scoops the yard once a week for dog poo. Jacob cleans the kitty box every day. They unload the dishwasher whenever I'm busy and don't have time. I just informed them recently that I am no longer going to remind them to do chores. They are old enough to see when things need to get done, so I'm taking those off my management list. We'll see how things go (a checklist may be popping up in their future!).

Having children do chores starting at a young age is important not just for the relief of an adult's mental labor, but to teach them valuable life skills. And I'm not worried about my boys because they take over even more chores whenever John and I go away for a weekend or on a quick vacation. Last summer they cooked, did dishes, took care of laundry, and were completely in charge of the pets while we were away for five days in Branson, MO. I've also shown them how to do some basic meals and

Jonathon took an Intro to Culinary class in high school, so hopefully they won't starve in the future.

I'm confident they'll learn a lot more when they have their first apartment while attending college later in life. That's where I got a crash course in housecleaning, and let me tell you, my roommates let me know when I was slacking. Thank you, ladies, you taught me a lot!

John still works 50 to 60 hours a week, but he has always been in charge of organizing and cleaning the garage and trimming the lawn. He also loves winter (a crazy concept to me) and doesn't mind shoveling and snow blowing along with the boys sometimes.

When it comes to housework and cleaning, everyone has to manage things differently according to their financial and life situation. I like our combination of hiring out the deep cleaning and dividing more of the everyday or every week chores among the four of us. I know we'll still have some bumps along the way, but by just being aware that I no longer have to bear every responsibility and by thinking about things differently, I already feel relief and my mental labor in this area is on its way to being cut in half.

So, we're on our way to easier, more streamlined financial management. Our home repair and maintenance tasks are falling into place and becoming more automated. And cleaning and housework is no longer dumped on just one person's shoulders. We have hope for simpler home management. Now let's look at how to shop smarter for various items within the home and cut down on meal planning and creation.

# *Chapter Three*

## Shopping and Meals

**Shopping and Meal Planning**

Groceries. Weekly menus. Personal hygiene items. Pet food. Prescriptions. Clothing. These items are necessary for most households, but they don't magically appear when we need them, darn it!

For groceries and most personal items, you can always go the delivery or pick up route. In Central Indiana, I've used Shipt, a service that delivers things from either Target or Meijer. You simply select what you need online using an app or visiting their website on the computer. You pay an annual fee of $99, and orders over $35 are delivered for free. Prices on some items are slightly higher than what you would find in the store, although they have many things on sale each week. And then of course you need to tip your shopper.

This all may sound too expensive, but if you are often guilty of making impulse buys, you could come out even. I know I'm not the only one who runs to Target to buy a few things and ends up coming home with 20!

Grocery pick up services are also convenient and not as costly. Walmart offers free grocery pick up at many locations in the United States. Other stores charge around five dollars per order or a little more for expedited pick up. Most of these services are similar. You place your order online and select a future pick up time. Then at that designated time you pull into the parking lot and slip into one of the marked spots. From what I've seen, you are not expected to tip these shoppers.

I think these services are absolutely brilliant for many situations. When you're sick, it's wonderful to be able to stay home and rest, or at least just drive up to the store and sit inside your vehicle versus dragging your nearly lifeless body inside the grocery. And your fellow shoppers are probably grateful that you're not sharing your icky germs.

If either of these services had been available when my kids were little, you bet your sweet bippy I would've taken advantage of them! My nephew's wife had a baby right before Christmas and she recently posted on Facebook how relieved she was to be able to use Shipt and not worry about exposing her precious little girl to a bunch of germs. I hadn't thought of this benefit but it does make sense.

Once again, I know many people might be reluctant to try this service. When I first started to use Shipt, some of my friends wondered if the shoppers would be as particular about selections as I would be. Wouldn't they also make some errors? But I've found that most shoppers are as picky as I am, especially with produce. And if they are ever in doubt about something, they can easily text me.

They do make mistakes occasionally. I'll never forget the time I ordered a five- pound bag of rice and ended up with a 20 pound one. At least we didn't run out of rice for six months! But shoppers are human and most of these errors are not the end of the world.

Some of you may want to avoid paying anything extra for groceries. I get it. As winter was approaching recently, John and I started looking at ways for us to cut costs, since my husband's business slows down dramatically at this time each year.

I shop at Aldi, which has incredibly low prices for good quality food, and I am able to get 75% of what we need there each week. Even though it's wonderful, this store can't provide everything that a typical household needs. I used to order the remainder of our groceries online and have them delivered, but as I mentioned, it was a bit more expensive. So John volunteered to go to Meijer every week for us since he's not working as much. It's such a time saver and a relief for me to not have to go to two grocery stores.

*Lighten Your Mental Load*

Sharing the grocery shopping responsibilities with a partner or taking turns can be a huge help along with using the occasional delivery or grocery pick up option. But what about meal planning and cooking in general? This certainly requires some mental labor, but I personally don't mind it at all. I've always enjoyed cooking and have a variety of dinners that I rotate. I plan out easy meals that don't require a lot of time for weekdays or ones where I can throw things in the crockpot and let them cook all day. I save more elaborate dinners for weekends. And I give myself a break each week by making Friday our pizza or carry out night.

I realize that meal planning and cooking, especially for dinner, can actually be a burden for others. Although I haven't tried them, I've heard great things about meal planning services. These range from services like Plan to Eat, which provides a grocery list for you based on recipes you drag and drop online, to eMeals offering a huge variety of menus, all the way up to places like Home Chef that deliver recipes and all the ingredients right to your door.

You can find information on these and other meal plans on doughroller.com. In a 2019 article, the site stated, "If your normal weeknight dinner plans involve dining out or scrounging around the fridge for leftovers, meal planning could be exactly what you need. A great meal plan can help you eat well while saving money."[17] It went on to share information about 10 meal planning services so you can figure out what might work best for you and your family's needs and budget.

Another great tip I've heard in recent years is to make all dinners ahead of time either once a week or once a month and freeze them. You can create your own meal plans and do the shopping for these or use one of the aforementioned services. I have friends who love doing this every Sunday, every other Sunday, or the first Sunday of the month. It's a relief for them to

---

17 https://www.doughroller.net/smart-spending/9-best-meal-plans/

come home after a busy workday and throw something in the oven or on the stove. You obviously need a lot of freezer space for this option, but it works well for many families and cuts down on the mental load of meal planning and preparation.

To help me with suggestions for various meals, I now have a "Meal Ideas" section on our dry erase board that is stuck to the front of our refrigerator. When anyone in the family is craving a certain dish, they can simply write it on the board to help me with my planning. Rifle Paper Company also offers a farm fresh weekly meal - planning pad on anthropologist.com that keeps a week's menu in one place. It also comes with a tear away shopping list you can add to as needed.

Now that we've discussed how to help with the mental labor of grocery and personal care shopping along with meal planning for humans, let's move on to our furry friends.

Although there's a variety of pet food at most grocery stores, we are quite particular about what we feed our cats and dogs and prefer to get their food from a pet store. This is of course another avenue where you can order items online. In my research, I've seen many advantages for going this route.

First of all, it's nice to have one less errand to run and to save time and gas. Some people live in more rural areas where the nearest pet store is maybe 30 minutes or more from their home. Second, lugging around huge bags of pet food can be challenging if you have a disability, back issues, or if you're just plain tired from a long day at work. Through Amazon and other online sites, you can set up a recurring delivery that comes to your front door so you never have to lift heavy bags for long distances or worry about running out of pet food ever again. Remember, automation is a wonderful tool to relieve mental labor!

Third, you'll find a greater variety of pet food and supplies online and often save money. Finally, ordering pet food online is a nice way to send a gift to someone or make a donation to an animal shelter.

Even with all of these advantages, I personally don't shop online for pet food. We only live five minutes from Tractor Supply Company, which is literally right beside Aldi. Their prices are rock bottom because we are members of their Neighbors Club. Our dogs and cats are small and we can easily store a month's worth of food for all of our pets thanks to having large bins with lids. The bags of food aren't too heavy. I enjoy seeing everyone at this store once a month, plus they are great community supporters. So this is one load that is actually quite light for me. With a little bit of research and planning, you can discover the best options to help slash your labor in this area as well.

One mental load that I *am* working to decrease, however, is prescriptions. My husband John gets three a month from two different pharmacies. Many people are now switching to getting their prescriptions via mail or delivery. This is incredibly helpful, especially when you have the same prescriptions from month to month. Most pharmacies, even small local ones, offer this service for free for regular mail or no rush delivery. The advantages include:

1. Not waiting in line at the pharmacy.
2. Cutting you out of the middle and having prescriptions sent to the pharmacy right from your doctor.
3. Easy transfer of existing refills.
4. Saving time and gas.
5. Avoiding exposure to germs in crowded pharmacies.

With the larger pharmacies, by using a simple app on your phone, you can receive notifications when your prescription is ready, choose a delivery method, upload a payment method, and even track your prescription.

If you're not tech savvy, you can still get prescriptions mailed or delivered to you and often save money. Many insurance plans have a smaller copay when ordering a 90-day supply for home delivery. Talk to your doctor and ask for a 90-day supply with the appropriate number of refills. Ask him or her about generic options as well.

To get things started, you can bring in your prescription to the pharmacy, submit it by mail, ask your doctor to call, fax, or e-prescribe it, or fill out a refill submission form by hand.

I'm working with my husband to switch to this option, because it feels like one of us is always running to our local pharmacy at least every week or two. Even though we get automated reminders of when a prescription is due for pick up, this errand gets pretty old and definitely adds to our load.

By the way, there are similar systems for your pets' prescriptions. Some sites offering this service are chewy.com, drsfostersmith.com, 1-800PetMeds, and PetCareRx. You may also save money for your furry friends' medications this way!

So now we're hopefully making less trips to various stores for both human and pet food along with personal hygiene items. We're streamlining meal planning and not visiting our local pharmacy or veterinarian office as often. Let's move onto another basic need.

Many women enjoy shopping for clothes, although that's not true for all of us. I know I personally look forward to my annual "girls shopping trip" every fall at an Indiana outlet mall or in our beautiful historic downtown. It's also fun for me to take an hour or two every couple of months to explore one of our unique local thrift stores. I'm a huge fan of hunting for garage sale bargains as well.

Some clothes shopping, however, can become part of the mental load. I think it's especially tough when you start to have children and are forced to shop more often as they grow into different sizes. Even if you have a baby shower or two and loving relatives that enjoy buying your little one some clothes (my mom was always thrilled to pick up items for the boys) it's not uncommon to have to shop every couple of months for clothes when you have babies and/or toddlers. And if you're not careful, this can get expensive.

One Godsend for our family was having friends who were kind enough to pass along their children's clothes when they were done with them. I made sure to do the same in return for our friends who had boys younger than ours.

I also love the recent popularity of children's resale and consignment shops. As one brilliant blogger recently said on lifehack.org, "Kids grow quickly, so why would you want to spend $25 on a new shirt or $40 on a new pair of jeans when your son or daughter is going to outgrow them in a year or less?[18]" It just makes so much sense to buy gently used clothing for your growing child.

I tried to take less frequent trips to stores and garage sales for my kiddos by planning ahead. We were fortunate that my sons are only 16 months apart, so most of Jonathon's clothing could easily be passed down to Jacob. I always browsed in the children's section whenever I shopped in a thrift store and I paid attention whenever I saw garage sale signs advertising children's attire!

Thanks to buying clothes a size or two bigger and storing them in our attic, I was nearly always prepared for those days when one of the boys would slip on a pair of pants to discover they had become "high waters" - pants you could easily wear to wade in water. Sometimes I missed the mark on estimating a future size, but since I spent very little on clothing, it wasn't the end of the world when the boys didn't get to wear something I had purchased.

I did like to buy my sons some brand new clothing on occasion, mostly for special events or holidays. I visited our downtown children's boutique for those items a couple of times a year, and I was glad to help a local family-owned business.

I may be starting to sound like a broken record, but online shopping can yet again be a huge help to help reduce the mental load of shopping for children's clothes. I've recently started shopping online more often for my

---

18 https://www.lifehack.org/articles/lifestyle/20-amazing-benefits-thrift-shopping-you-probably-never-expected.html

teenagers' socks and underwear. It's quicker and often cheaper than going to a nearby department store.

According to an industry survey, parents spend two-thirds more money shopping online and three-quarters more time shopping online than their non-parent counterparts[19]. "Parents, especially working parents, are arguably the busiest adults in history," explained trends expert Daniel Levine of Avant-Guide Institute. "Anything that makes their lives easier is going to be preferred over a similar activity that is more time-consuming." One mother shared that she prefers online shopping because she can take her time and get exactly what she wants, versus being in a rush when she is shopping in person with kids in tow.

Since our boys are now teenagers with jobs, we still provide them with the basics, but they buy most of their clothing.

No matter how you shop for children's clothing, the key is to do all you can to reduce your number of physical trips to make your purchases each year, whether it's a thrift shop, department store, children's boutique, or local garage sales. Try to stock up on items that are a size or two ahead when possible for kiddos who are still growing quickly. See if online shopping can become a part of your mix, at least for basics like socks, underwear, undershirts, etc.

So what about us grownups? For those of you who just don't like shopping or feel inept at putting together outfits, you can always sign up for a clothing subscription service. These businesses have popped up in the last couple of years for both men and women and are quickly becoming a popular option to simplify our lives. You can get started with any of them by completing a survey with questions about your sizes and preferences. According to an October 2018 Business Insider article, clothing subscriptions can be incredibly useful for anyone who wants the freedom to explore trends

---

[19] https://www.racked.com/2017/5/23/15625998/childrens-shopping

or even go-to styles without much commitment, financial burden, or closet space [20].

"If you like using them, chances are you're going to really like using them. If you don't, you can cancel and continue the search," wrote Mara Leighton.

Both men and women have a variety of services to choose from. Some offer clothing for rent, purchase, or a mix of both. The services offer all types of clothing, from dressy, to business, to business casual, to casual. Some carry athletic attire and undergarments. Others feature accessories and jewelry. You can discover services for plus sizes all the way down to extra small sizes.

One of the first companies to offer this kind of service was Stitch Fix, a personal styling service that makes getting dressed easier by delivering clothes you'll (hopefully) like straight to your door. You simply keep what you want and send back what you don't. You pay a styling fee each month that gets applied toward clothing that you purchase.

These services make a lot of sense for people who just don't enjoy shopping for their clothes or feel like they need help with styling decisions. A word of caution – remember to watch your budget and make certain you're only buying things you truly need. Most of us wear 20% of our clothing 80% of the time and would be much happier with fewer wardrobe choices than we have now, according to Becoming Minimalist [21]. But you'll never realize that until you test it out.

The site goes on to say that the fashion industry invents *false need* by boldly declaring new fashion trends and colors for every changing season. But you don't have to fall for their tricks. Find your favorite timeless fashion and start playing by your own rules.

---

20 https://www.businessinsider.com/womens-clothing-subscription-boxes-2018-7

21 https://www.becomingminimalist.com/thin-closet/

I've finally learned to buy high-quality classic pieces, many of which I can actually find at a thrift store. By avoiding trends, investing in timeless clothing, and taking care of what we already own, we can greatly reduce the number of shopping trips and online purchases every year. And that alone can lighten this mental load up to 75%!

**Some Thoughts About Online Shopping**

OK, I've mentioned online shopping a lot. And I'm not done talking about how it can help us by any stretch of the imagination. But I think we need to be careful about relying on this option exclusively for shopping.

Yes, it's a great tool for reducing the mental labor in this area of our lives. However, I never want to get to the point where I use it exclusively. Here's why.

1. Supporting and getting to know your local businesses is vital for your town or city to thrive and grow. Those family-owned shops are often the ones who donate silent auction items for local nonprofit events. They help downtown districts, which are dying in many cities and towns throughout the US, remain strong to attract both residents and out-of-town visitors on a regular basis. These business owners typically live in and care about your community.

2. Your local big box store also helps your community despite being part of a chain. Walmart, Target, Home Depot, and many other large stores offer grant and sponsorship opportunities for communities where they have a presence. Your local nonprofits often rely on these just to keep their lights on and to fund other operating expenses.

3. It's wonderful to get to know employees at your local store. I actually look forward to seeing Dana, a long time cashier and employee, when I go grocery shopping at Aldi every week. We are about the same age and even have the same birthday. We've shared a small connection and some laughter

during most every transaction. I also enjoy talking to the owners of our local organic meat store. They're terrific with all of their customers.

4. You'll find more one-of-a-kind items when you shop locally versus online. I love to shop in our local downtown for at least some of my Christmas gifts because I know my family and friends will be pleasantly surprised. It's wonderful to explore these shops with my girlfriends as well.

5. In some cases you save money by shopping locally. Unless I'm in a huge hurry and simply can't run to the store, I try to always compare prices before purchasing something online.

6. Online shopping may not be the best for the environment. Yes, we want to decrease the mental load, but not at the expense of our planet.

I heard a story about this very topic in November 2018 on National Public Radio in a segment called "Super-Fast Shipping Comes With High Environmental Costs." [22] M. Sanjayan, CEO of Conservation International, stated, "While online shopping does have a smaller carbon footprint than traditional retail shopping, it's only really better for the environment if you don't get rush delivery."

"By basically checking… 'take your time and deliver this to me in the best method possible'… the trucks are going to be filled to the brim with goods when they're being sent, and the company's going to use the most efficient way to get it there," he continued.

Amazon Prime even gives you credit if you select the "no rush shipping" option on your orders. It's also wise to be careful with your purchases so you're not constantly returning things, which creates a negative impact on our planet thanks to more vehicle trips.

Finally, I realize not everyone has Internet access at home. Of course you can always use data on mobile devices, but many people have a limited data plan. And some people aren't comfortable with technology and don't use

---

22 https://www.npr.org/2018/11/26/670991367/super-fast-shipping-comes-with-high-environmental-costs

anything that would enable them to shop online - computer, tablet, mobile phone, etc. My mother falls into this category. I'll talk about how I help her later on.

I believe it's smart to use a mix of both in person and online shopping. You can essentially automate the processes with both, even if you're just making monthly notations in a paper planner or calendar. Put a dry erase board up on your refrigerator where *everyone* can jot down household items that need to be purchased or request certain dishes they'd like to have for dinner. By the way, this dry erase board is also a great place to note leftovers in your refrigerator so you don't forget about them and cut down on food waste.

We've thoroughly covered how to reduce the mental labor involved in shopping for various items we all need for the home. It's time to talk about the people and pets who live in those homes, including our partners and children, and how to decrease the mental load in managing their various schedules and activities.

## Chapter Four

### Partners, Kiddos, and Pets

**Partnerships vs. Boss/Secretary**

Sharing your life with someone can be amazing. I've been married to my husband John now for over 20 years and couldn't ask for a better partner. He's there for me during the good and bad times in my life and vice versa. We definitely have our disagreements, but I'm fortunate to call him my best friend.

Some of these disagreements start when we move away from our partnership to more of a boss/secretary relationship. For example, I became extremely irritated when he used to call and ask me to set up a doctor, vehicle oil change, or other appointment for him. Number one - I was already doing my own work and managing my own life. Number two - I didn't know his schedule, so how the heck did I know what worked best for him?

After one tense conversation, I finally blurted out, "I am your wife, not your secretary!"

Of course, in a marriage or other partnership, we're supposed to (and should) support and help each other. When this relationship is working properly, it helps smooth out the bumps that we encounter along life's journey.

But let's face it, there are still tasks we should do and need to do for ourselves, unless we are sick, disabled, or dying. Allina Dizik wrote about how this should work in a relationship in a January 2018 article on workingmother.com.

"We don't pull each other into the other's mental load. We each buy our own toiletries. We each call our own relatives. We each research our own winter boots, and—in general—act like independent adults," she stated [23].

Dizik goes on to say that they try to skip reminders. "Instead, I calmly focus on my own tasks, while letting my spouse focus on his. If a task was previously assigned to him, then I try (with all my might) to forget about it. Vice versa."

In previous chapters we discussed some ways to divide up the mental labor of home management, chores, and shopping. But there's another overwhelming category that requires help as well - scheduling. It's not so bad when it's just two adults. But it becomes a whole 'nother thing when you add kids to the mix.

**Kiddos and Pets**

I love being the mom of two boys. Nothing makes me happier than when they are both home goofing off with their friends. Our mudroom is full of shoes and our house is overflowing with laughter, heavy footsteps, and sometimes a strange smell or two. Food disappears almost as quickly as I serve it, along with any and all beverages.

In just a few short years we will be empty nesters. I've learned to cherish the time the four of us have under this roof as well as our vacations and long weekend trips. I will miss Jonathon and Jacob's dancing and other antics.

What I won't miss, however, is the mental labor of their various schedules, which started literally when they were born. Newborn babies have to go to the doctor frequently for checkups during the first two years of their life. The American Academy of Pediatrics and the American Dental Association both suggest children start visiting a dentist by age one. The

---

[23] https://www.workingmother.com/experiments-in-offloading-mental-load

American Optometry Association recommends taking a child to their first eye appointment at six months of age and approximately every two years after that.

The next thing you know, it's time to sign them up for preschool or kindergarten, unless you decide to go the homeschooling route, which simplifies some areas of life but complicates other areas, as we will talk about later. Soon you're scheduling time for children to get together with their friends, since nowadays their friends aren't often in the same neighborhood, and keeping track of - and probably helping with - homework and after school activities.

Time Magazine wrote about a book published by Susan Walzer in 1996 called *Thinking About the Baby* in a December 2016 article. It stated that Walzer found that women do more of the intellectual, mental, and emotional work of childcare and household maintenance [24]. They do more of the learning and information processing (like researching pediatricians). They do more worrying like wondering if their child is hitting his developmental milestones. And they do more organizing and delegating like deciding when the mattress needs to be flipped.

The article went on to share what this might look like in a typical household through the following "note":

*Honey, I'm going to be out of town for the weekend. Remember that the pediatrician's number is on the fridge, we're expecting a package on Saturday and you should intercept it if you can, Susan has a sleepover at Amy's later that night and I wrote the address in your calendar, Scotty has a piano lesson on Sunday at 10 so don't let him sleep in, the number for Mikey's Pizza is programmed into your phone, and the flower bed out back could really use some weeding if you're up to it.*

---

[24] http://time.com/money/4561314/women-work-home-gender-gap/

I do believe that some things have improved for women since Walzer's book came out a couple of decades ago as I've shared earlier. But we still need some help to reduce this mental labor of scheduling. A great place to start is to not add a bunch of stuff to the household calendar in the first place.

We definitely want our children to be healthy, so skipping the recommended frequency of doctor, dentist, and eye appointments isn't a good answer. We want to nurture their friendships and help them experience the joys of play dates and birthday parties (although we *can* say no once in a while, especially if it places a huge burden on the family overall. Your child will live, trust me). We can make some changes, however, in their homework and after school activities.

According to Psychology Today, children should have no more than ten minutes of homework per day per grade level [25]. Thankfully my children's homework has pretty much followed those guidelines. And I can count on both hands the number of times my sons have needed our assistance in getting homework completed. But in other school systems, that's often not the case, as illustrated by my friend whose middle school-aged daughters have to stay up late some evenings just to get everything completed - and who often require their mother's help since their father travels frequently.

Most parents don't realize they can speak up to teachers and schools about excessive homework. We have the right to educate teachers and principals about the research surrounding it. We also can create allies by speaking with other parents and banding together to address homework with local schools.

Even if children are bringing home the right amount of homework, they still require our help to be successful, especially at the start of their school career or the school year in general. Make certain there is a quiet designated

---

[25] https://www.psychologytoday.com/us/blog/the-squeaky-wheel/201110/how-much-homework-is-too-much

spot in your house for homework. If your child is struggling with something, try to guide them through the issue by asking them questions or referring them to their notes or textbook. Help them create a good system for homework management from the start so you don't have to constantly worry and remind them.

If your kiddos still need some help, of course you should assist them. I've always had a knack for English class and writing, so I'm happy to proofread and guide my sons in these kinds of assignments. However, they don't want my help in math! When you're not strong in a subject, see if a sibling or friend can assist your child.

We have a great free resource in Indiana thanks to the Rose-Hulman Institute of Technology. Thanks to Ask Rose, students in grades 6-12 can get math and science homework assistance via phone, email, or chat. God bless these awesome college students! I've also seen other homework help lines available in different states throughout the U.S.

Let's move on to the other category of after school stuff - extracurricular activities. For this topic, I am forever grateful that I bought a book called *Simplify Your Life* by Elaine St. James in the late 1990s. I read – and re-read – that book and committed many sections of it to memory before I became a parent.

One terrific tip she shared was to keep your children involved in only one - or at the most two - extracurricular activities per semester. I remember discussing this with my husband at the time and he agreed with me 100%. Once we had children we followed that rule. Our boys joined Cub Scouts when Jacob was in second grade and Jonathon was in third grade. With weekly meetings and monthly camp outs, along with special events, that one activity kept all four of us busy. I volunteered as an assistant den leader and John helped lead the annual Pinewood Derby every spring for the pack for years. Jacob began to take piano lessons when he was 10 and fortunately we found a good teacher less than a mile away to make things easier.

Both boys lost interest in scouting right before high school, but Jacob has been involved in either choir or jazz band each semester of middle and high school. Jonathon was a part of the high school's coding club before starting work at Pizza Hut. As a senior, he starts each day with classes on site, but goes to a career center every afternoon.

Many of you may be reading this and shaking your head in disbelief. A lot of extracurricular activities are good for kids, right? We want to expose them to a variety of interests so they know what they will enjoy now and later on in life. Plus, these activities keep kids busy so they don't get into trouble.

Extracurricular activities are great, no doubt about it. Even though my boys gave up scouting years ago, it still affects their lives most every day. But children need free time.

To decide what works for your children and family, start with the basics. Is your child getting the right amount of sleep? Shortchanging them on sleep due to an activity isn't good for anyone in the family. The American Academy of Sleep Medicine recommends 10-13 hours of sleep for children ages 3 to 5; between 9 and 12 hours for kids up to age 12; and 8-10 hours until age 18.

Do they have time to play every day? Playtime is important for children to reduce stress and grow problem solving and critical thinking skills. Of course this time definitely changes when kids reach their teen years. For both of my sons, playtime involves creating elaborate films with their friends. Yes, video games are part of the mix, but thankfully that's not all they do.

Is there time every day for you to gather together to have dinner as a family? Stop laughing. This can be achieved with some creativity and flexible dinner times, even if it's only three or four evenings a week. I remember once reading that Mitch Daniels, a former governor of Indiana, was able to have dinner with his wife and daughters at least three times a week. If his family can do this, I think most anyone can. Having dinner together as a family is beneficial for children on so many levels.

Does your child have the right amount of time needed to complete homework and visit with friends? Doing well in school should always come before extracurricular activities. And nurturing friendships is vital for anyone no matter what their age.

Get to know your children to gauge how much structure each one of them thrives upon. For example, my son Jacob enjoys being involved in more activities than his older brother Jonathon. He enjoys being "on the go" most days between visiting friends, participating in jazz band, and working. Jonathon prefers more alone time, although he certainly likes socializing a couple of times a week outside of work and school and driving up to a county park to practice his archery.

Don't forget self-directed activities. Even though Jacob still takes piano lessons, his teacher works with him on whatever pieces he selects. One week it could be jazz band tunes, the next it could be a new song he's discovered that he wants to explore. I've never seen a child practice so willingly, and I know it's because he is guiding his musical path.

What about helping children find their interests? Shouldn't they be involved in numerous activities so they learn about themselves? Not necessarily, according to Dr. Susan Newman, a social psychologist and author of *The Case for the Only Child*.

In fact she recommended something entirely different: Step back. "Most children find their level and their interest if they have the time to do it," Newman said [26]. "My advice to parents is always to understand your child and see what limits he or she has or doesn't have."

There's one other part of the family that has activities at least every year or every few months, and that is our pets. At the minimum, your pets require an annual check up to make sure they are doing well and are current on

---

26 https://childmind.org/article/finding-the-balance-with-after-school-activities/

shots. They may also need to be groomed every two or three months like our three dogs.

Every veterinarian office I've dealt with sends out either a snail mail or email reminder for our pets' annual checkup, which helps to automate the process. I typically take the dogs all together on one appointment, then the cats on another six months later. With five pets total, this greatly reduces the number of trips we need to take each year. The appointments may be a bit chaotic, but it's worth it.

I am fortunate that our groomer is literally across the alley from our house. I have a reminder set up in Outlook to schedule the dogs' "styling" appointment every three months. All three of them can go together at the same time, which makes life so much easier.

Not everyone has such a simple set up, however, and it may be difficult to coordinate grooming appointments while working out of the house full-time. Mobile grooming - where someone comes to your house and does all the grooming in a specially made van - may be a fantastic option for many households. Some veterinarians make house calls as well. This is great for busy families or elderly pet owners.

Many large pet stores offer grooming as well, making it easier to get your dog all gorgeous outside of work hours

Hopefully this section has given you some great ideas to make homework and activities easier for your children and pets as well as your overall family. Let's explore one last option for your kiddos that might be right for them and for you.

**Homeschooling**

Homeschooling has gained popularity in recent years for good reasons. In this section I'll talk about how homeschooling *may* help your family and your mental load - and how it may not.

My niece Melissa has been homeschooling her children for almost seven years. She is a stay at home mom to six children ages 12 and under. Yes, this woman deserves a medal!

Melissa was initially only going to homeschool her children for kindergarten after she realized how complicated it was to load her kids in the car to drop Lily, her oldest child, off for preschool and to load them all back up again a few hours later to pick her up. She also felt that Lilly would not do well in an all-day kindergarten program, especially because she was still napping.

"I bought a kindergarten book with phonics to test it out," Melissa said. "We liked it so much we've kept going."

Melissa believes she can give her children the best education thanks to homeschooling.

"In general schools are not what they used to be. I don't think kids learn like they used to. Teachers have so many kids and have to follow so many rules they can't discipline like they should - it is a challenge," she said. "At home I can control our schedule, what we do, their values, and what they are learning."

Melissa stated she's fortunate that it's fairly easy to homeschool in her state of North Carolina, whereas in other states it's more difficult.

"Here you have to register, keep records of year end standardized tests, and keep attendance. As far as curriculum, you can use anything," Melissa stated. "But, homeschooling is challenging and stressful in the beginning. I tried different curriculums before finding what was right and spent a lot of time on the Internet."

Melissa does most of her teaching in the morning. While her younger children nap in the afternoon, her older kids do assignments and reading while Melissa works out. She loves the flexibility of homeschooling especially with field trips and vacations, since the destinations aren't as busy. She and her kiddos also get together with other homeschoolers through a co-op group. Melissa stated that homeschooling does make life easier if you have a big family.

"Home school families tend to be large. It's not unusual to see four plus kids. When you have a lot of children, by homeschooling, adding another one isn't a big deal."

I asked her if it's possible to work at home or work part time outside the home and homeschool. Melissa knows one homeschooling mom who is a nurse who works weekends, while another mother works nights.

"Some work from home, but it is a challenge. You still have to teach them. You have to block time to teach. You can't bounce back and forth."

While homeschooling can decrease your mental load in some ways, it can add to it in others. As Melissa's kids have gotten older, four of them are now involved in extracurricular activities that start in the late afternoons, making the entire family's schedule more complicated during the evenings.

"Something is going on in two or three different places between 4 and 8 p.m. on the weekdays," she said. "And Saturdays are full of sports. If they were in a traditional school, I would not have them involved in as many evening activities."

To help lighten her family's mental labor and schedule, she and her husband are talking about pulling her kids out of some of their activities starting next year.

One final advantage of homeschooling is allowing your kids to get up when they want to on weekdays. "My kids are so much more productive when they get enough sleep," Melissa stated.

If this option sounds appealing and you're planning to start a family or your kids are still babies and/or toddlers, I would encourage you to do further research to see if homeschooling can be beneficial for your family and if it can help decrease your mental labor in the future.

**Keeping Track of it All**

We've learned to set some boundaries with our spouse or partner. We're working to help the entire family breathe easier with various schedules. Now let's explore different ways to keep track of everyone's activities.

My first rule on this topic is don't place this load on only one person. And I'm talking from experience here! Right now I alone handle this rather large category of mental labor. But that is already starting to change and will evolve in the weeks to come.

I'm currently processing information from the January 2018 blog I mentioned earlier by Allina Dizik. She started out this article saying, "I've been trying a new approach to achieve that coveted-yet-unrealistic idea of a 50/50 household. It's ambitious, but I don't care," she wrote. "The experiment? Let's creatively call it 'equal distribution of the mental load.'"

Dizik is a parent of two children and admitted in the article that her mental labor has greatly increased thanks to having kids. She and her husband started to share more of their family's mental load by splitting up tasks in a way that accounts for it. In other words, they don't just divide up the management of schedules and chores, they think through what is involved with each one from start to finish and assign accordingly. Dizik shared one example to illustrate this concept.

"He recently sent out our daughter's birthday invite, wrote the text and tallied the guests rather than asking me to write the text and keep track of the RSVPs while he physically sent the email," she stated. "It was a small battle, but I won."

Dizik also shared what she and her husband had learned so far in this process. She said that no day is perfect and working to distribute the mental load equally takes constant effort.

"There will always be new, unassigned mental loads that pop up," Dizik said. "You can't know the full extent of the mental load your partner carries. The tit-for-tat can make you feel like enemies."

Finally, Dizik and her husband learned it's a strategy that needs to be constantly recalibrated.

"Our biggest takeaway: The mental load is never going to be perfectly distributed. I'm OK with that," she wrote. "But on days that we succeed in more equal divvying-up, I find myself feeling lighter and with more energy to devote to dreaming about yoga retreats."

Dizik has already inspired me and given me hope. I took one small step in unloading my mental load of scheduling a couple of weeks ago. Jacob's piano teacher had texted me about a change of time for his lesson that day. Thanks to this book, I shared his cell phone number with her and let her know that from now on she can communicate with him directly for any schedule changes. He's 16 now and driving himself to and from his lessons. He can certainly handle texting or calling his teacher for any changes and vice versa.

No matter how you're dividing up the mental labor of scheduling, it can be helpful for everyone to use technology as often as possible to streamline the process.

**Family Organizing Apps**

I didn't even know family organizing apps were a thing until I saw an advertisement for Cozi in Family Circle magazine. Then again, I'm technologically challenged at times.

According to the ad, with one shared calendar, everyone adds events and sees who's doing what. Cozi will notify others and send reminders so one person doesn't have to. The app helps you share the grocery list, chores, and a meal plan. It says it is easy to use from any mobile device, tablet, or computer.

The full-page ad revealed something that got me excited – color-coding! Each family member has their own color so you can tell at a glance who needs to be where and when. You can even assign a color for your pets. I color code things all the time for my business, so this makes perfect sense to me for use in the home.

Obviously your children have to be a bit older in order to use this technology, but with the knowledge preteens and teens have nowadays, chances are they'll do better with this than you will! Even if your kids are little, it's great to use an app like this between you and your partner if you have one.

Other apps you can try include Google calendar, Hub Family Organizer, and Wunderlist.

As I write this I'm already planning our family meeting where we'll all discuss Cozi, download it, and get on the path to splitting up this mental load of scheduling!

You can also use your smart phone to help with schedules. For example, every time you schedule an appointment such as a doctor visit, set up calendar reminders in your phone to ping you two days before and again when it's time to leave.

### A.I. Assistants

What the heck are A.I. Assistants? A.I. Assistants, or artificial intelligence assistants, are application programs that understand natural language voice commands and complete tasks for the user. You may know them better as Amazon Echo, Google Home, Sonos Beam, and others.

My sons and I bought my husband an Amazon Echo for Christmas, but we soon realized it was a perfect gift for everyone! Whenever anyone remembers something that needs to be put on the grocery list, instead of having to write it down, we just ask Alexa (the Echo) to put it either on the

Meijer or Aldi list. My husband uses it as a reminder to take his medication every evening.

In the past when my computer was shut down and one of my sons asked me to take care of something for them the next day, I would write it on a sticky note and put it on my laptop so I could throw it onto my Outlook calendar first thing in the morning. I realize I could put Outlook on my phone, but just haven't gotten that far yet.

Now I can just say, "Alexa, remind me at 9 a.m. tomorrow to transfer money from Jonathon's checking account to his savings account."

I haven't even fully explored all it can do, but I'm quickly realizing that Alexa can dramatically improve the mental load of our household. And I'm not alone.

"Think about some of the things that Alexa (and Google Assistant and Siri) can do. Set timers. Take reminders. Remember where the keys are for a later date. Order groceries and household items when they need re-stocking. Turn kitchen appliances on and off," said Sophie Charara in a November 2018 article in The Ambient [27]. "Sound familiar? Alexa and other voice assistants are already well on their way to becoming 'CEO of the household.'"

Charara stated that these devices are an even greater help for families when more than one person is using them for household reminders, tasks, and scheduling. I'm just on the cusp of realizing what this means for my own personal mental load, and I'm almost giddy! The three men in my house love using technology, so I have a feeling they'll embrace using Alexa more and more in the months to come.

---

27 https://www.the-ambient.com/features/alexa-mental-load-household-1201

## But We're Not Comfortable With or Able to Use Technology

Once again, I realize not everyone is tech savvy and we're not all equipped with computers and other devices for the home. You can still make the scheduling and reminder process a breeze with a good old-fashioned hard copy calendar. I've seen some great dry erase and paper ones at numerous big box and office supply stores. You can either use weekly or monthly ones. Just be sure they are large enough for writing down various activities and locate them in a central spot in your home where everyone can easily use it and see what's going on. And don't forget to use the color - coding system!

Another technique to help organize your schedule or your family's schedule is bullet journaling. This new trend is extremely popular at the moment. Apparently it has triggered over 3 million Instagram posts. I don't actually use this system, but I understand that entries are tagged with bullet points, dashes, and other graphics so you can see various categories at a glance.

Ryder Carroll created this unique system. By updating it daily, "you learn how to get rid of things that are distracting you and add things you care about," Carroll said in a March 2019 Good Housekeeping article. You can log in your daily to do list, monthly calendar, notes, long-term goals, and more.

I decided to view the five-minute tutorial available at bulletjournal.com. True to its word, I got the hang of it in five minutes. This looks like a wonderful system for managing your schedule and it can also help you weed out the unimportant things in your life. Apparently it's a lot of fun once you get the hang of it! I would recommend it for anyone who wants to keep track of things on paper versus using technology.

I used a dry erase calendar on the side of our refrigerator for years to keep track of what everyone was doing from month to month. It was yet another sanity saver for me, although I was the only one who wrote things on it. But of course that was before I learned all of my new "reduction in mental load" skills!

Woman's Day Magazine shared another good tip in its "Ease Your Mental Load" article in February 2019. The article recommended that family members take charge of their own schedules with personalized chalkboards for important events like big tests and due dates. It went on to say that kids will learn responsibility and time management and parents will get a much needed break from constantly reminding them of activities.

No matter what family calendar technique you use, whether it involves technology or an old-school calendar placed in a central location, I'll end this chapter stressing that it's important to follow one rule.

"As your children get older, teach them it is their responsibility to get their events and deadlines on the family calendar as well," said Lara Galloway, a business coach to moms and co-author of *Moms Mean Business*[28]. "Doing so reduces lots of stress for everyone in the family, helps avoid forgetting things and eliminates stressful last-minute scrambles to make things happen."

---

[28] https://www.care.com/c/stories/5250/finding-the-family-calendar-app-that-works-fo/

# *Chapter Five*

## Transportation

### Getting from Here to There

Transportation is one hot topic these days. And unfortunately for most of us, it sometimes adds to our mental load. Let's examine various modes of daily transportation, the mental labor associated with each, and ways to make that labor easier.

### Vehicles

*"Cars are money suckers,"* is something you can quote me on.

We *love* our cars in the U.S. For the first time in my life I can say I do adore mine. I drive a 2007 Mini Cooper S stick shift and it's my dream car. However, owning one or more vehicles can definitely create mental labor. We're paying the price on many levels for being so dependent on our cars.

According to City Lab, in 2010, Americans drove for 85 percent of their daily trips, compared to car trip shares of 50 to 65 percent in Europe [29]. Longer trip distances only partially explain the difference. Roughly 30 percent of daily trips are shorter than a mile on either side of the Atlantic. But of those under one-mile trips, Americans drove almost 70 percent of the time, while Europeans made 70 percent of their short trips by bicycle, foot, or public transportation.

There are numerous reasons for this difference and it's negatively impacting the United States on many levels, including infrastructure that

---

29 https://www.citylab.com/transportation/2014/02/9-reasons-us-ended-so-much-more-car-dependent-europe/8226/

struggles to keep up with handling all of those vehicles, a nation that is gaining more weight by the decade, and environmental problems. This could be a topic for a whole other book (in fact others have written them!).

While city planners and various community leaders have been gradually making changes by creating more trails, better connectivity for biking and walking, and alternative transportation methods, we still have a ways to go in this and other countries.

My own city just completed a river walk not far from my house that connects to other trails. It helps me in my training walks for my half marathons. I'm fortunate to live just nine blocks south of our downtown and am able to walk to many places. In fact, I've walked to work in the past when I was employed by the City of Noblesville and Hamilton County.

Things are slowly changing in the United States, and I'm excited about that fact. I truly would love to ditch my car in the future, even though it is quite awesome. But I know I'll still need a vehicle for at least another couple of decades, and so will many of us who don't live in the heart of big cities.

Just like our homes, vehicles require maintenance, upkeep, and repairs. Unlike our homes, however, most vehicles don't appreciate. We all know that as soon as we drive a car off the sales lot it instantly goes down in value. Plus, most of us have to buy cars more often than houses.

Think of how many cars you and your family have owned in your lifetime. Think of all the money you've spent on car payments and, of course, the interest on vehicle loans. Consider car insurance as well. On second thought, maybe you don't want to go there. I'm not even brave enough to do it.

If you really want to get depressed, think about all of the car repairs that have cost hundreds if not thousands of dollars at a time. Unless you're mechanically inclined, this number won't be pretty. Now consider the new tires, brakes, batteries, etc. that you have to fork cash over for even on pristine, well-maintained vehicles. Not to mention the oil changes and fuel.

Now you probably understand my quote that kicks off this section. The average person typically gets a different vehicle every 4 to 8 years. That process alone involves many steps, including visiting different sales lots, doing test drives, loan approvals (unless you pay cash), going to the license branch, etc. Even if your car has no major issues while you own it, you still have to do the regular maintenance of oil changes, tire rotations, new tires, battery changes, and tune-ups. And of course you have to get fuel often, unless you drive a hybrid or electric vehicle.

That's a lot of stuff to keep track of.

So what can we do to relieve the mental load of vehicle ownership? First of all (don't laugh) you can strive to pay cash versus taking out car loans. We started both of our sons out on this path and we hope it continues. Jacob saved up and paid for his first car with cash. We gave our older son Jonathon our old minivan. He has been saving up for a different vehicle and is close to his goal.

We're teaching them to continue this process and we hope it will become a habit for a lifetime. By putting money into savings each month versus paying back a car loan, they can get a newer, better vehicle every couple of years thanks to the amount they save and whatever they get from selling their current car. Dave Ramsey, the well-known financial guru I mentioned earlier, talks about this concept often. I love it because you can avoid the hassle of taking out loans and the interest involved.

John and I have not been able to do this yet, however, we are taking another approach to help with the mental load of owning a vehicle - keep your current car for as long as possible.

John's car is essentially his office. He travels around Central Indiana and beyond to visit peoples' homes to sell them gutter systems, garage floor coverings, insulation, and other products. We talked long and hard in the summer of 2014 and decided to purchase a new hybrid vehicle with the intent of keeping it 10-12 years or longer. We've never regretted this decision.

We're approaching the halfway point this year and I'm confident we'll reach our goal. Why? First of all, we have been meticulous about this vehicle's maintenance. We never miss a recommended tune-up, tire rotation, etc. thanks to postcard reminders sent to our home. John works to keep it clean inside and out. We also can finally keep both of our vehicles in a garage when we are home, helping their exteriors stay in tiptop shape. As a result, John's vehicle looks - and more importantly, drives - almost exactly like it did when we first bought it.

We're also grateful we took the plunge and paid a little more for a hybrid. Before we owned one, John made numerous trips to get fuel every month. This of course ate up both time and money. Thankfully now both have been cut in half, simplifying the mental load significantly.

Our friend Dan owned his Toyota Corolla for 20 years followed by a Honda Civic for 11. He's had his Acura now for 10 years. He followed the same good maintenance routine. We never heard him complain about unexpected car repairs and he rarely goes through the hassle of having to find and purchase a different vehicle.

Of course, unexpected issues can happen even with the most well maintained cars. This puts quite a load on our shoulders as we try to sort out the chaos for our families and our schedules. Belonging to a roadside assistance program such as AAA or utilizing or purchasing a warranty when you buy a car can help lighten the load. It's reassuring that help is just a phone call away if you ever need it while you're on the road.

If you or your partner aren't handy with vehicle repairs, it's good to ask around and get to know someone who is strong in this area. I was fortunate to be friends with one of the maintenance men for Noblesville City Hall years ago who happens to be a whiz at some car repairs. He often saved me and many other people both time and money.

Not friends with someone who is mechanically inclined? Ask around to find a good, honest mechanic. Try to find a place that's either close to your home or workplace, which saves a lot of hassle. The mechanic for my Mini Cooper is just two blocks from our home, and they even offer loaner cars you can use during major repairs.

My final tip in this area is to automate things whenever possible. Our car insurance is taken directly out of our checking account every month. I do every single thing that I can online with our state's bureau of motor vehicles versus visiting our local license branch.

Try to combine your maintenance as often as possible, such as getting your tires rotated during the same visit for an oil change.

If you go to a grocery store once a week, make it a habit to also fill up your car at the same time, since many large chain stores have gas stations nearby. In fact, some are owned by the same company, so you can accumulate points by joining their rewards program to save money at either spot.

With some planning, automating of tasks, and doing things a bit differently, you can cut your mental labor of car ownership in half.

**Public Transportation**

Perhaps you live in a large city with good public transportation and you only need one car or you can ditch a vehicle altogether - my dream someday! Not owning a vehicle can lighten the mental load in one respect but add to it in another.

Going "car free" offers many benefits. You'll save an average of $700 a month thanks to no car payments, insurance, maintenance or repair costs, parking fees, and fuel. You'll probably walk or bike more often, which is terrific for your health. And by taking a bus, subway, or train, you can sometimes (if you are seated) read or perform other tasks during the commute that you can't do when driving a vehicle.

Ride-hailing services like Lyft or Uber or even a good old taxi can help fill in the gaps when needed. But what if you need to take a vehicle a few times a year to perhaps go out of town to visit family or friends?

"Car-sharing services like Zipcar and Car2Go allow you to access a car when you need it, and not pay for it when you don't," said genyplanning.com

[30]. "If you only need a car a few times a year, this could be a cost-effective option."

This entire concept sounds pretty terrific. However, public transportation can add to your mental load due to a single factor – safety.

On the one hand, your chances of getting into an accident by taking public transit versus driving a vehicle are lower. If you ride the bus, you are about 60 times safer than in an automobile in the U.S., according to analyst Todd Litman's findings published recently in the *Journal of Public Transportation* [31]. If you travel via commuter or intercity rail, you are about 20 times safer than in an automobile. And if you hop on the metro or light rail, you are about 30 times safer.

On the other hand, you are more likely to be the victim of a crime or harassment, especially if you're a woman. According to the Washington Post, the public transportation systems in some of the world's largest cities are seriously unsafe for women [32]. Groping, lewd comments and sexual assaults are so common that even the "safest" of these systems — New York's — are nothing to brag about, while the least safe systems, in Latin America, are nightmares.

I don't live in a city that offers convenient public transportation. I only use it when I travel. So I had to do some research on the top ways to stay safe when taking public transportation. Here are the best suggestions:
1. Avoid isolated, dark stops. Brush up on the schedules so you know the more illuminated places to depart from or catch your train or bus.

---

30 https://genyplanning.com/2017/08/30/ditching-car-save-thousands/

31 https://cleantechnica.com/2015/01/05/truth-safe-transit-compared-driving/

32 https://www.washingtonpost.com/news/morning-mix/wp/2014/10/29/the-worlds-most-dangerous-public-transport-systems-for-women/?utm_term=.7d75808853b6

2. Keep your fair or pass ready in your hand to avoid opening up your wallet or purse.
3. Stay aware and pay attention to the people around you. Move to a different seat if necessary.
4. Make note of the last train or bus of the night so you're not stranded.
5. Don't say your name, address, or phone number out loud while taking public transportation.
6. Pay attention to emergency buttons and exits.
7. Don't walk home alone in the dark.
8. Guard your valuables and avoid taking naps on public transportation. Not only is this a way to stay safe, but you'll also avoid missing your stop!
9. If someone doesn't know your daily routine, share your route with a friend or family member.
10. Always have your keys ready to get into your house or apartment before getting off at your final destination.

It's a shame to have to think about all of these things when taking public transportation, especially if you're a woman. But it's the reality of the world we live in.

I have one question that pops up after thinking through these facts, and I'm sure I'm not alone. Is going "car free" and taking public transportation still worth it? I asked this question to one of my clients, a young woman named Jenny who faces this reality every day thanks to living and working in downtown Indianapolis.

"I grew up in major east coast cities with trains and busses and then I went to grad school in a college town with a well-equipped bus system, so I have never had to learn to drive," Jenny said. "Walking, carpooling with friends, and public transportation have always been a simpler and more cost-effective solution. I now live in a smaller city with very limited public transit - still without driving. I handle errands outside of walking distance with ride share services like Uber and Lyft or rides from friends. This is obviously more expensive and less convenient than public transit, but still ends up costing me less monthly than owning and maintaining a car. It also saves me the headache of car ownership (searching for parking, stopping for gas, maintenance issues, traffic accidents, etc.). Even though a bus schedule or a ride share app might not always be as reliable or expedient as your own car, I have never found myself truly unable to get where I need to go. And if things are ever running a little behind schedule, that just means there's time to catch up on emails or enjoy a good book!"

"As a young woman, there have of course been instances where I've been uncomfortable because of a ride share driver or someone on public transportation," she continued. "But I have been fortunate to never find myself in a bad situation and always take common sense precautions such as checking in with friends, keeping my keys handy, etc. That is also simply an unfortunate reality for women in the world we live in and I refuse to limit myself because of it. I have never felt I'm at any higher risk on public transportation or in a ride share than anywhere else. Especially living in a downtown area with limited parking and more difficult navigation, I still find it's a huge advantage to not have to worry logistically or financially about a car."

I think Jenny answered my question beautifully.

In conclusion, by relying less on vehicles and more on walking, biking, and being alert and smart when taking alternative transportation, the mental labor of figuring out how to get from here to there on a daily basis can be reduced by up to 75%.

# Chapter Six

## The Mental Load in the Workplace

**Work Overload**

Talking about the mental load in the workplace may not make much sense. As I mentioned in the beginning of the book, if we're at work, we're getting paid to organize and perform tasks, right? Well, yes and no.

At work, some of the mental load includes all those little steps you take to uphold the smooth operation of your team that may or may not fall within your job description, according to Leah Ryder in a September 2018 Trello blog [33]. It's "remembering" work like:

11. Quick check-ins to see if others are keeping up their part in your projects.
12. Doing the legwork to book meeting rooms, generate video call links, ensure attendance, take notes, and generally facilitate communication.
13. Keeping up team culture with things like birthday card signings and after work event planning.
14. Being the formatting guardian on team reports so they're cleaned up for manager review.
15. Always digging up the data reports because you know how to use the software or have the account login.
16. Keeping the coffee pot full if your team is co-located, or if you're not...
17. Always being the first remote team member to break the ice and wish everyone "good morning" on team chat.

---

33 https://blog.trello.com/mental-load-invisible-work-stress

Some people enjoy components of this mental labor in the workplace. I loved being the one responsible for various celebrations in my department years ago while working in Noblesville City Hall. Bringing joy to others through organizing potlucks, decorations, desserts, sign creations, songs, birthday cards, etc. was a pleasure. I had various systems in place to help make all of these tasks quick and easy. I used Outlook to remind me of every special occasion and I stocked up on birthday cards and decorations thanks to my nearby dollar store. I created sign-up templates for potlucks and checklists for people to see who had signed a birthday card and who had not. I've always enjoyed writing, so creating a silly song or poem to make someone feel special is second nature to me and often took only minutes.

I realize, however, that not everyone enjoys this or other types of mental labor in the workplace. For some, taking this load on willingly or unwillingly often adds to the stress of each workday. And that's not good for an employee, a team, or the workplace as a whole.

To solve this dilemma, tasks and behaviors that fall outside of a job description should be taken care of equally among the team. Ryder stated these include keeping your team updated on your work at a regular cadences, keeping your owned items in project management tools or tracking up-to-date, knowing what budget or materials you need for your work to get done and being responsible for getting those requests fulfilled, and taking turns for planning team culture activities like birthdays and holidays.

"When team management is everyone's role, it can help each member grow professionally and build solid relationships that will pay off in spades for both your current to-do list and your future success at work," Ryder wrote. "Take some time to confront that elephant in the room and lift the invisible work weight off of your and your team's shoulders."

But what about the mental labor we do get paid for? At times this can certainly be overwhelming, especially when those sneaky little tasks from home or our personal life have to pop up during our workday and crash into what we're trying to accomplish for our job.

I turned back to my brother Mark for some great tips on how he manages this combination. Mark uses the Tony Robbins system to reduce his mental labor for both his work and home life every day. He captures all of his tasks in the morning and puts them into "buckets" to simplify things.

"For example, I'll have my insurance business bucket, my Expo Design bucket, my health bucket, and other buckets," Mark said. "Then I prioritize each bucket. For example, Expo may have 12 things that should be done but three *absolutely need* to get done. I star those three things and when they are done at the end of the day I get a sense of accomplishment."

He sets himself up to win every day thanks to his morning routine. Mark stretches and meditates every morning, does a gratitude sheet, and tries to study at least 5 to 15 minutes to improve himself. Two days a week he does a mastermind group where they talk about their wins of the week, accomplishments, and what everyone needs help with. A mastermind group is a peer-to-peer mentoring concept used to help members solve their problems with input and advice from the other group members. This concept was defined and explained by Napoleon Hill in his book *Think and Grow Rich*.

"I have managed my mental labor by always improving who I am and what I do," Mark stated. "I also manage the load by trying to make myself healthier. Your health affects your mental labor. I try to drink and eat healthier and exercise. I also work to manage my anxiety."

I love Mark's advice and it makes great sense. However, my brother is now a grandfather and doesn't have children in the home. So he doesn't face the challenge of balancing work and parenting responsibilities anymore, a problem that adds to the mental load of mostly women who work full time on an almost daily basis.

Workplaces need to evolve to give BOTH men and women more balance and flexibility to avoid burnout. We must change the mindset that women are always the ones who need to manage the household, take time off of work to be with sick children, etc.

According to Business Wire, fathers continue to be judged negatively by colleagues at work for taking care of issues at home, leaving women to take on the bulk of family responsibilities [34]. Yet men want to be partners in parenting – in the 2015 Modern Family Index, working dads indicated they want more time at home and 46 percent experienced burnout at work due to lack of family time.

Today's working fathers are also hungry for change and even more likely than working mothers to crave evolution. The 2017 Modern Family Index report showed working fathers are nine percent more likely than working mothers to wish their employer offered more flexibility and 32 percent more likely than mothers to give up a 10% raise for more family time.

Business Wire shared that workplaces must help decrease the mental labor for working parents.

"Now is a more important time than ever to break out of traditional male/female stereotypes – both at home and at work," said Bright Horizons CHRO Maribeth Bearfield. "The fact is that for most employers, much of their most valuable talent in the workplace is playing double duty as manager of family life as well. By providing supports to working women, they can help open up mindshare that can contribute even more to the workplace. And by creating environments where men are encouraged and valued for taking advantage of work/life supports as well, workplaces can start to catch up with the culture this generation of working families demands."

I'm fortunate to be able to work from home now and to have teenage children. When they're sick it's nice to be with them, but I know they can deal with most illnesses fine by themselves if I have to leave for a meeting. Parents with smaller children, however, have no choice but to figure out who

---

[34] https://www.businesswire.com/news/home/20171220005984/en/New-Research-Shows-"Mental-Load"-Real-Significantly

is going to be home with a sick child and miss work. This can cause tremendous stress and juggling of responsibilities.

Employers should strive to offer better options to support fathers and mothers in the workplace. One of my girlfriends, Cassandra, gets three sick days a year and three weeks of vacation. That's it. No matter how long she works at this office, that's the most she's ever going to be able to take. So Cassandra often works when she's ill to save her days just in case one of her young sons gets sick due to her husband traveling often. This certainly isn't good for her and for those who work near her.

Cassandra's not even allowed to work from home on occasion, which is an option that would help her situation immensely. When her sons are healthy, she also has to take time off of work for their doctor, dentist, and eye appointments. Cassandra likes to take a couple of half days to volunteer at their schools as well. When you add all of this up, it doesn't leave a lot of time to take a true vacation.

If her workplace offered more flexible work hours, telework options, and even just a couple more sick days, Cassandra's mental load would decrease tremendously.

I hope Cassandra's workplace wakes up and makes some changes soon. Thankfully, other employers are doing more to support working mothers and fathers.

"Inherent to being a great place for all is the recognition that employees are three-dimensional people with lives outside of the office that affect their performance in it," wrote Scott Healy in a February 2018 care@work blog. [35] "True employers of choice understand this, and that's why many recognized as 'Best Companies' are maximizing human potential by taking care of employees' families. Actively addressing work-life conflict helps employees

---

35 http://workplace.care.com/best-companies-family-friendly-benefits

stay present, productive and engaged – with peace of mind at home, they're able to bring their best selves to work."

More employers are offering generous parental leave policies, back up care for children and seniors, flexible working models, unlimited PTO (paid time off), and paid bereavement time for the loss of *anyone* in an employee's life.

This all sounds wonderful, but I'm sure many of you are reading this thinking, "I'm in a situation more like Cassandra's. How can I change the culture of my company or organization?"

Taking with other employees and working together to show your employer how these steps will actually help *them* can be a good first step. Healy ended his blog by stating, "While the benefits, policies and perks vary, two things are clear: 1) Companies that demonstrate how much they value their employees are valued in return; and 2) Family care benefits are proven to reduce absenteeism and turnover, while improving organizational health and talent acquisition. As Fortune points out, being a Great Place for All is more than a badge. The elements that make you a great place to work also add up to faster growth and stronger returns than the competition."

Start by talking with your HR department if you have one to see if they're willing to make a few gradual changes, backing your points up with evidence from Healy and many other online sources - there are numerous articles out there! Do you have a competitor that has implemented some of these great practices? It might not hurt to point these out - tactfully - to your employer.

I know of course that some places won't budge on their policies no matter what evidence you show them. If you're in this situation and are desperate to reduce your mental labor in the workplace, perhaps it's time to start looking around for a new job with a better environment for working parents. If this is the route you decide to take, try to find a place close to home as well if you have a long commute. This is another great tip from Elaine St. James' book *Simplify Your Life*.

I've either worked from home or close to it since the late 90s and I doubt I'll ever change that pattern. It's been a relief, especially with the occasional emergencies that inevitably crop up with children and now, my mother. Working close to home saves a tremendous amount of time and money. You spend less time in traffic and less money on fuel and meals. I loved walking home for lunch when I worked for the City of Noblesville or Hamilton County. I not only saved money, but it gave me terrific exercise on an almost daily basis! Plus the walks were a great stress reliever during crazy workdays.

When looking for a new job, another great way to reduce the mental load is to find a position with fewer hours. We've all heard that the 40 hour work week is dying, but some places recognize the importance of work/life balance and consider full-time employment to be 35 to 37 1/2 hours a week. Many local government workplaces follow this concept.

In summary, working together to more evenly distribute the "hidden" tasks, prioritizing what absolutely needs to get done while striving to be our healthiest selves, working with others to help our workplaces implement better policies for working parents, or just looking for and hopefully becoming an employee of a place that already offers these policies can reduce the mental load at work by 50% or more.

## *Chapter Seven*

### Birthdays, Celebrations, Holidays, and Vacations

**Birthdays**

I think birthdays should be celebrated, no matter what your age. However, I don't believe every single birthday should be celebrated in an expensive and complicated manner, especially with children.

When I was growing up, I had probably three or four birthday celebrations with a group of friends. Most of these were simple parties in our house with around five girls to celebrate the "big" birthdays. As I got older, slumber parties became the norm. I celebrated my sweet 16 with both boys and girls at a local pizza place. All we needed were video games, pizza, and each other - and we had a blast.

The rest of the time we just gathered with family over dinner for my birthday, or any other relative's birthday, and had cake. I fondly remember many of those celebrations.

I'm not sure when things started to change, but it amazes me today how some parents will go all out for every single one of their child's birthdays, year after year.

We followed in my family's footsteps for our sons. Jonathon and Jacob have had about three or four birthday parties each with friends. Some of these we held away from home at sites such as an indoor inflatable place, video game establishment, or bowling alley. The rest were simple celebrations at our house or going out to dinner with just the four of us at a favorite spot. In fact, one of my favorite celebrations at home was a movie party for Jacob's 13th birthday. His friends arrived dressed as their favorite movie character, and I taped a small piece of paper with a movie title on each guest's forehead. Throughout the evening Jacob and his friends had to ask each other questions to figure out what their movie was. We had pizza and then everyone watched a classic PG-13 film. Jacob still talks about how much fun he and his friends had that evening!

I kept things as simple as possible for every celebration. I made sure to always have invitations on hand for the kids to give to their friends at school, and most of the time we invited maybe five or six boys at the most.

Now, I'm not here to ruffle any feathers. If you have the time, money, and creativity to plan big celebrations outside of the home every year for your kids' birthdays, wonderful! I'm sure many parents enjoy the planning and implementation of these parties immensely.

I'm also pretty certain others aren't in this camp, but they feel the pressure from society to go all out every year. Libby Hudson Lydecker summed this up well in an April 27, 2017 article from Real Mom Daily [36].

"...the pressure started to get to me, and I found that I'd begun to dread the impending birthday seasons," she wrote. "And I started to re-think the whole endeavor."

Lydecker accurately stated that a lot of us throw the big parties because, of course, we love our children and want to make their day special. We want to make them happy. But she also pointed out we don't always have to go over the top in order to reach this goal.

"I say it's time to give ourselves a break. Let's stop making it so damn complicated. Hey, if you want to throw an over-the-top party and you have the means, then go for it. But at the end of the day, our happiest childhood memories are more often the simple things," Lydecker said. "The happy feeling after a long day playing outside, the comfort of a cake that Mom made just for you—and the feeling of being truly celebrated on the day of your birth."

I want to encourage you to rethink your birthday celebrations if they are creating a big mental load in your life. You might discover that the simpler

---

[36] https://www.realmomdaily.com/why-are-we-going-overboard-on-childrens-birthday-parties/

get-togethers make your child just as happy as the big ones, if not more so! And you'll be breathing a sigh of relief at another part of your mental load decreasing.

## Other Celebrations

Birthdays aren't the only reason for parties of course. From weddings to anniversaries to graduations, we should gather with friends and family to mark these wonderful occasions and celebrate the ones we love. But these celebrations are often getting out of hand as well, creating almost painful mental labor in some instances.

As I mentioned earlier in this book, I've been happily married to John for 20 years. However, this is not my first marriage. I was briefly married to a man we'll call "Tom" in my early 20s. We were married in a church for that wedding. We had a huge reception for about 125 people in a nearby gymnasium with a catered dinner, bar, DJ, and a big wedding cake. We had a nice rehearsal dinner the night before, and beautiful flowers that cost hundreds of dollars. My wedding dress was around $500. We each had five attendants who of course either had to rent tuxedos or buy bridesmaid dresses. We also had a ring bearer and flower girl. A professional photographer captured all of the important moments.

I remember being in tears on more than one occasion during the planning process for my first wedding. I won't go into all of the reasons in order to protect certain individuals but managing all the people involved in this wedding was sometimes challenging. I remember being quite stressed in the months leading up to the ceremony. I'm fairly certain the whole affair cost both of our families around $15,000, which I understand is actually not a bad amount these days!

This is a huge contrast to my second wedding. John and I planned our wedding in one evening as I rode with him while he worked in his tow truck. We decided to get married in our home in December of 1998, since his brother was going to be in town from his Air Force stint over in Germany. A dear friend of ours made the wedding cake as a gift to us, which was still absolutely delicious when we pulled some of it out of the freezer a year later! Other friends and family pitched in for a potluck dinner.

My brother's business at the time offered rentals, so we were able to get tables, chairs, and cocktail tables along with linens and some dishes for free. A wonderful rabbi that we met at a wedding a few months earlier married us in the doorway between our parlor and our living room. We had about 40 guests. My dress cost around $100 and John's tuxedo rental was about $75. His brother Ron was the best man and he wore his dress uniform from the Air Force. My niece Melissa was my maid of honor and she wore her prom dress from the previous spring. My sister Vicky and Ron handled the photography that evening.

It was definitely a simpler ceremony, and it helped that this time I was marrying the right man! But all kidding aside, when our wedding and reception were over, we probably heard at least a dozen times how much people absolutely loved the whole event. "That was one of the best weddings I've ever been to," they said.

I was never stressed in the planning and implementation of this wedding. By keeping everything simple, I enjoyed the whole process from start to finish.

Once again, I don't mean to make anyone angry. Some men and women have dreamt about their weddings and how elaborate they can be since they were small children. Some people love to plan and execute other large celebrations as well. If you have the money and all of that brings you joy, go for it!

If the thought of these bigger celebrations, however, makes you want to go bang your head against the wall, then good Lord, don't do it! It can be so difficult to not do the same thing that your friends and family do for these occasions. You may have that feeling that it's important to "Keep up with the

Joneses." But if these events are more than you can handle financially, emotionally, physically, or even spiritually, why put yourself through it all?

A couple of years ago my husband and I attended a graduation party at one of our local arts venues. My friend and her children made the appetizers as well as the cake. They served soft drinks, lemonade, and water. It was such a simple, special afternoon that I decided right then and there to do the exact same thing for my sons' future graduation celebrations. I literally just put the down payment check in the mail a week ago for this venue for Jonathon. While there is still going to be some work involved for this graduation party, it's definitely going to be simpler for us to host it in this beautiful, cost-effective place close to home.

Yes, celebrations are wonderful and I absolutely love them. But we all need to reassess how to honor and show our love to friends and family. Sometimes the simpler route can be even more meaningful for everyone involved. Take some time to look into your heart and trust your gut when planning your next celebration. You may end up with treasured memories and a lot less mental labor!

**Holidays**

I have a friend named Linda whom I've been close to now for over 23 years. Even though she lives an hour away from me, we often catch up with each other during a Sunday afternoon chat on the phone. I know her so well by now that I can predict what our conversation will revolve around right after Thanksgiving - her seasonal decor. Linda goes all out with her Christmas decorations. I've never actually seen them, believe it or not, although I think it would be well worth the drive sometime to visit her house during the holidays. Every year it takes her about three days to get her decorations out and put into place. I'm sure it's a beautiful sight worthy of a magazine!

Her husband Don likes to decorate for a different holiday – Halloween. Apparently their yard is the talk of the neighborhood every October. This year he even built a "mausoleum!" Once again I wonder why I haven't I made the drive down there more often. I'm sure it is a spooky, spectacular scene.

I used to decorate a lot for each holiday before I had the boys. For decades, my mother taught people how to make beautiful ceramic creations and I inherited a lot of her gorgeous pieces of art. After I had Jonathon, however, I didn't even bother to put up a tree that first year, since he was born in early December. I knew I would be overwhelmed after entering the world of parenthood and I didn't want to worry about decorations.

Over time, I realized I didn't have the energy to go back to my old ways. Whereas Christmas decorating used to take an entire day in my household, now it takes approximately three hours. In addition to our Christmas tree, I put one or two holiday decorations in each room of our house. Neither my husband nor I have ever put up Christmas lights. We enjoy the twinkling lights of our Christmas tree that are visible through our front parlor window.

I put out maybe two or three decorations for the other holidays, depending on how busy I am. One year Jonathon was in charge of Halloween and he did a great job with some skeletons! I'm happy with all of my holiday decorations and relieved that they don't require a lot of time and energy.

My point is that Linda and Don genuinely enjoy the effort that goes into decorating their house for various holidays, which I think is awesome! I know other people who feel a great deal of satisfaction and pride when spending many hours or days transforming their homes. My hat goes off to them and I love seeing the results of their hard work.

For me and some other folks, however, it's preferable to keep things simple for the holidays. I finally learned to resist the pressure from neighbors, magazines, home and garden television shows, and those aisles and aisles of decorations that pop up in the stores every year starting in August!

I know this isn't easy to do. Have you ever seen the movie *Christmas with the Kranks*? While this is not an Oscar worthy film, it does make a good point for this topic. The movie features a middle-aged couple whose daughter is not coming home for the holidays. To lift their spirits, they decide to essentially skip Christmas and go on a cruise instead. No decorations, no holiday party, no presents, no fancy Christmas cards.

Unfortunately, their neighbors, friends, and coworkers aren't supportive of their decision. Soon they are practically shunned by everyone they know, especially their neighbors who all decorate to the hilt both inside and out for Christmas.

While the movie certainly went overboard, I recognized a grain of truth while watching it. We are surrounded by messages every year, especially through advertising, to make the holiday season incredibly magical and to transform our homes into gorgeous wonderlands. We are pressured to find the perfect gift for every family member and friend, to bake dozens and dozens of gorgeous cookies worthy of Pinterest posts, to throw and attend lots of parties, and to send out stunning Christmas cards that should be framed.

While some people thrive and enjoy this, it can create a stressful, painful mental load for those of us who don't.

I've gradually been decreasing my mental labor for the holiday season in recent years. I now bake one or two favorite Christmas cookies either right before or on Christmas Eve. My husband and I have talked to our families and we've all agreed to only buy presents for children, our spouses, and for my mother and John's father. I stopped sending Christmas cards in the mail about five years ago and instead create beautiful online e-cards that I send to close family and friends.

Even with a smaller Christmas list, shopping is still a bit overwhelming, especially because the grant world tends to get busy right before the end of the year. I finally spoke up and asked John to pick up a few presents this past year. Not only was he happy to help, but he also did a wonderful job with his selections!

Guess what? Despite all of this, our friends and family are still talking to us. They still love us. In fact they probably appreciate us more because we're not so frazzled at the end of every year! And the holiday police have never, ever shown up at our door to arrest us.

There's a popular saying currently and I think it's appropriate for this section. When it comes to the holidays, "You do you!" If it brings you joy and you've got the time, money, and energy to go all out and make your home amazing and the envy of the neighborhood during Christmas time, go for it. If you want to stick up a little Charlie Brown tree in the corner of your dining room and declare it to be your one and only Christmas decoration, so be it. If you want to fall somewhere in between, that's wonderful!

If everyone did what brought them the most joy every holiday season, I think there would be a lot less Scrooges and a heck of a lot more happy campers who are relieved to carry a lighter mental load.

**Vacations**

Merriam Webster defines a vacation as "a period spent away from home or business in travel or recreation." When we're on vacation, our mental labor should be practically nonexistent, don't you agree? But unfortunately that's not always the case, especially in the weeks and days leading up to and after that time away.

Traditionally in our family, I'm always the one who puts the actual vacation days on everyone's schedule, makes the flight arrangements if that's our mode of travel, plans out what we need to pack, shops for toiletries and other necessary items, and guides everyone on what to put in their suitcases. I typically find someone to take care of our house and pets as well. If we're traveling by car, I always take the appropriate vehicle in for an inspection to make certain it's ready for the road.

When the boys were little, this whole process was, of course, even more complicated. I had to consider things like formula, portable highchair seats, pack and plays, diapers, baby food, wipes, etc. I packed every item of clothing, containers of wipes, burp cloths, small toys... just remembering it all makes me tired. I can recall loading up our minivan and being amazed at all the crap we had to haul around. Even if we were just going away for a long weekend, it looked like we had enough stuff to last us for a month.

And no matter what stage of life we're in, once we get back home there's the process of unpacking and doing mountains of laundry, something I pretty much handle all on my own as well. I learned long ago to take that last day at home before going back to work just to catch up with everything.

Once again, I've always been an organized person. So, I've never considered decreasing my mental load when it comes to planning our trips or recovering from them. But I'm sure other women are in this same role and are absolutely overwhelmed every year. While I couldn't find ideas about how to relieve this mental labor in my research, I'm sure the same "divide and conquer" approach can work for pre-and-post-vacation steps for couples. Thankfully my sons are older so they now do their own packing for trips. I'm sure if I asked John to take a vehicle in to our mechanic before every vacation from now on he be happy to do so.

Fortunately, when I've left and I'm truly on vacation, I've always been able to actually escape from work. I've never been required to check my work email or voicemail. Now that I'm self-employed, I plan on continuing that tradition. I wish everyone else could do the same. Too often I see or hear of people who still have to check in to work either because it's required or they feel some sort of obligation. I know all too well that some people do this in order to avoid a backlog of work on their desk upon their return.

One of my heroes, Randy Pausch, author of *The Last Lecture,* was one heck of a busy guy when he was alive. In addition to inspiring millions of people around the world thanks to his incredible attitude after being diagnosed with pancreatic cancer, Pausch was an American professor of computer science, human–computer interaction, and design at Carnegie Mellon University. He co-founded the University's Entertainment Technology Center and he started the Building Virtual Worlds course as well, which he taught for 10 years. He consulted with Google on user interface design and also consulted with PARC, Imagineering, and Media Metrix. Pausch founded the Alice software project as well.

Oh yeah, and he had a wife and three small children. So you can imagine that this man had a heck of a lot going on. But I was impressed to read in his book that when he took a vacation with his family, he truly focused on them and got away from his work.

"Take time out," he wrote. "It's not a real vacation if you're reading email or calling in for messages."

Some of us, especially in America, don't even take the vacations they deserve. According to bigthink.com, Americans are taking off far less time than other countries [37]. Americans often look at vacation habits in countries like France and Spain with a mix of envy and amusement (both have 36 days/year of mandated paid vacation), and even the United Kingdom has 28 days of mandated paid vacation for full-time employees.

The reasons for this surprising behavior vary. Some people simply don't have paid vacation time, or enough paid time. Others worry that they'll be seen as a slacker. And some individuals can't afford to travel or do anything special with their time off.

With both women and men feeling the exhaustion of mental labor now more than ever, we need to change these habits quickly. Planning, preparing for, and unpacking from vacations can - and should - be done by more than one family member. And when we are traveling, or even enjoying time at home during a "staycation", most of us should be able to avoid emails, voicemails, and other work reminders, unless you're running a country or something like that. Then I get it.

I started this book during my time off right after Christmas last year. Like a lot of people, I typically take a vacation between Christmas and New Year's Day. Even though we don't travel during this time, I thoroughly enjoy the

---

37 https://bigthink.com/david-ryan-polgar/americans-dont-take-enough-vacation-that-may-be-changing-says-new-study

more relaxed atmosphere at home. My mental load is light and my cares are few. I find that the week recharges me and helps set me up for success for the new year. I never check work emails during this time, which allows me to truly escape and relax mentally and physically.

I'd like to end this chapter by encouraging you to do all you can to take the time you need to escape the pressures of everyday life. Not only will it help you reduce your mental labor, it will improve your health and increase your happiness. I think we all can agree those two things are most important in life!

# Chapter Eight

## Volunteering, Church Activities, and Hobbies

**Volunteer Work**

Doing volunteer work, especially with family or friends, is such a rewarding experience. I've been volunteering in one way or another ever since I was a teenager doing projects with my youth group at church. I was blessed to learn about a marvelous co-ed service fraternity when I attended Indiana University thanks to my friend Joni. I pledged my sophomore year and Alpha Phi Omega made my college experience that much better.

I've continued to volunteer for various organizations as an adult. John and I gave a lot of time and service to the Cub and Boy Scouts back when our sons were members. Our family has enjoyed doing service projects at church and delivering meals in the community every other month or so.

People volunteer for numerous reasons. GVIUSA.com listed 17 excellent ones in their January 2019 article. They include [38]:

18. It's good for your health and career.
19. It helps you learn new skills and make an impact.
20. Volunteering gives you a real world experience.
21. It enables you to give back to a cause you believe in.
22. You can empower others.
23. It helps you travel responsibly and make excellent connections.
24. Sometimes you can even learn a new language!
25. You become a stronger part of the community and explore more of your world.

---

38 https://www.gviusa.com/blog/17-excellent-reasons-to-volunteer/

26. You gain a whole new perspective.
27. It's inspirational and fun!

Volunteering always has been and always will be a part of my life. However, if I'm not careful, it can also contribute to my mental load. I'm sure I'm not alone. Sometimes volunteering can feel like a job. When we start to cross that line, it's often draining.

I've finally learned to draw my boundaries. I'll never forget the time an organization reached out to me regarding grant consulting. This board member and I exchanged some pleasant emails. I was eager to meet with her to discuss the possibility of her dog and cat shelter becoming a potential client. I sent her my rate sheet along with some possible dates and times for our meeting. Imagine my surprise when she replied, "Oh! I thought you'd want to volunteer to do this because you love animals so much." I had a good chuckle on that one. I tactfully replied that I already volunteered by assisting Noblesville Main Street with their grants and that my time in that capacity was full.

I know when a volunteer opportunity is right for me when I'm excited to do the work week after week or month after month. For example, I'm currently mentoring a young woman who wants to eventually become a great consultant. Alice is an absolute joy and I love watching her grow and giving her advice. I like seeing her emails and texts or getting her phone calls.

Please don't ever volunteer to do something that you dread. I don't care how much pressure someone is throwing at you, eventually another person will step up to fill that role. One thing I avoid at all costs is event planning. I'll work my little patootie off during an event as a helper, but don't put me in charge of that sucker. The last time I was in charge of an event and was on site to implement it, my lip broke out in cold sores and I almost got a migraine headache. Nuh. Uh.

I do realize there are some situations where you are "volun-told" what to do vs. being able to pick and choose how you want to volunteer. One example of this is parents who have children involved in swimming. I have adult family members and friends who spend many weekends working as timers, head timers, security guards, hosts, clerks, or other positions to help their children's swim meets run smoothly. Without parents volunteering, these events simply couldn't happen. However, the people I know enjoy this volunteer work (most of the time!) because they love to support their kids.

Another thing to avoid is joining something just so your name is on the roster. It may look impressive that you're on six different boards of director lists, but if you're not giving your all for those organizations, it's not a good fit for you or them. I remember last year I tried to volunteer for my Old Town neighborhood association, the Southwest Quad Group. Some issues began popping up with my mother and soon I was missing various meetings. I finally had to tell the group that I just wasn't giving them my best and that I would step aside.

What's one surefire way to tell that volunteering is adding to your mental load? Consider whether your volunteer responsibilities are keeping you up at night. It's my belief that we have enough things in life that keep us staring at the clock at 3 a.m. Our volunteer work shouldn't be one of them.

As I stated earlier in this book, I serve on two boards of directors. These are working boards - that is, they don't just simply govern but its members work to plan and implement different events throughout the year. Between both organizations I probably donate an average of 10 hours a month. Not all of it is a picnic of course, but most of the time I enjoy it because I believe in the missions, the people work hard and are fun, and the events help me learn and grow.

In summary, if you pick and choose how often and on what level you volunteer and make certain that what you do brings you joy versus stress, chances are volunteer work may not ever have to be part of your mental load.

**Church Activities**

Church activities are pretty similar to volunteer work. In fact, they mostly consist of volunteer work except for when we attend service. Even then, some of us volunteer by providing the music, ushering, performing some readings, being altar servers if you're Catholic, or being the leader who manages all of this at a certain service every weekend. I'm sure there are other roles I'm forgetting!

It's so easy to get sucked into volunteering in many ways in your church. And you can't blame pastors or other staff members for doing all they can to recruit people for various positions. Just like with the collection basket, churches often face the 80/20 rule, or Pareto principle, when it comes to finding people to perform the duties of various ministries. If you've never heard of this rule, it means that 20% of people do most of the donating and the volunteering in an organization or church. To put it in another way, 20 percent of a congregation typically does 80 percent of the work.

If you're in that 20%, church activities can sometimes add to your mental labor. I remember going on a women's retreat over 20 years ago at my church. It truly was one of the greatest weekends of my life. However, I was surprised at the end to hear us all get recruited to plan the next retreat to take place the following year. Back then, I literally had no free time - and this was even "BK" (before kids.) I had to tell them I could join them, but it wouldn't be for at least three months.

Planning this retreat required weekly meetings. Some of us, including me, had to create 30-minute testimonials. And of course putting on the retreat itself meant long hours and little sleep. It definitely contributed to my mental load, although I didn't realize it at the time. Thankfully, the entire experience was enjoyable overall and I gained many friends, some of which I am still in contact with decades later. Without these lovely ladies, I never could have survived the newborn baby and toddler days with my sons! They really were a Godsend, pun intended.

What can we do to help our church change that 80/20 rule if we are contributing too much and feeling that mental load? One of my favorite sayings is that God loves a cheerful giver. I don't think it pleases Him when we start dreading or dragging ourselves to perform certain tasks for our church. To keep church activities from contributing to our mental labor, we can help turn things around and get more people involved.

Mark McDonald wrote an excellent short article on this topic in July 2014 in Multi Briefs: Exclusive.

"I realized that the church now uses the 80-20 rule as a crutch," he said [39]. "It's an excuse for why churches can't do more or do ministry better."

McDonald stated that churches accept this because they keep asking the same 20%, they lack entrances into ministry positions, and they secretly dread training volunteers.

"We need to decide that our churches should have opportunities for everyone. And we need everyone to participate," he said. But how do we go about this?

McDonald shared three helpful tips. The first is to create "on ramps" for service opportunities. Churches need to have ministry fairs for recruiting and to instill in their congregations that people need to step up. And they need to demonstrate how to do it.

He also recommends limiting time in key roles. Churches need to keep the 20% from doing it all by implementing term limits. Setting a "rest period" for these roles encourages others to come forward. McDonald finally suggests creating an atmosphere of training, which is the key to encourage and motivate many people to take on the various tasks. Engaging all members will utilize spiritual gifts and talents.

I realize it's not always easy to work with church leaders to bring about these changes. You may not have the time or energy to work with them to

---

39 http://exclusive.multibriefs.com/content/why-20-percent-do-80-percent-and-how-to-fix-it-religious-community

implement the steps, or they may not even be open to them. That's when it's time to focus on yourself.

Let's go back to the steps we took with volunteer work. Do you feel good about the church activities you're participating in? Do you look forward to them or do you dread them? When these activities start to cause you more stress than happiness, perhaps it's time to examine these roles and figure out ways to gradually ease out of them.

Another area that creates mental labor in the church world is our children's religious education and/or youth groups. Just playing "parental taxi" can be challenging when we have to shuttle our children to and from religious classes, activities, and retreats. And of course, different age groups have different activities that all happen at - yep - different times! These activities naturally also need volunteers to help make them successful.

We definitely want to do all we can to strengthen our kiddos' spiritual lives. So how can we simplify things? My biggest tip in this area is to talk to other parents, get phone numbers, and set up lots of carpools! I did this for years and cut my taxi time in half.

When it came to supporting my kids' church activities, obviously I attended all retreats and events where parents were required. Other than that, I have to admit I was minimally involved in this area of life. Just like most people, I had a lot going on with my work, family, and volunteer activities outside of church. I just didn't have the time to show up week after week for a youth group or religious education class.

However, I did figure out one way to help, and that was by contributing food for meetings! By signing up to bring a side dish every month or so for our church's youth group, I was at least helping to make part of the evening successful. I simply had to mark my calendar for when it was time to buy a veggie tray, various desserts, a fruit tray, etc., then remember to drop the food off that following Sunday before the meeting.

Returning to more adult church activities, for about five years I participated in one of our church choirs, which had been a dream of mine ever since I was younger. I loved singing and serving at mass in this capacity. I made many friends, most of which I still see every once in a while and chat with.

However, once my mother moved closer to us, something in my life had to go. Unfortunately, I gave up being part of the choir, but I still serve as a reader during mass once or twice a month. I also distribute meals to families in our community every couple months through another ministry. Other than attending mass every week, this is the most I can do at this stage of my life. And I realize that's OK. I know I'll do more later on when I'm an "empty nester." Sometimes we just can't do it all, and we shouldn't even try because it would create a huge strain on our mental load.

Remember, God loves a cheerful giver. This simple saying should serve as a guide whenever we consider adding a church activity to our life and help it not contribute to our mental labor.

**Hobbies**

Like vacations, hobbies should take us away from our mental load, right? Absolutely, but sometimes if we're not careful, hobbies can get complicated and add to our mental labor before we know it. They're kind of sneaky that way!

For example, Ryan and Katie, two of our dearest friends, signed up a bunch of guys, including my husband, to play in a softball league years ago. It was a blast. John and I looked forward to Friday evenings from spring through fall, and our sons spent their earlier years at the ballpark watching their father play softball. Most everyone had little kids, and soon they all became friends and enjoyed time on the nearby playground during the games. The softball wives loved getting to know one another and became friends as well.

The entire experience was so much fun. But I know it was also a lot of work for Ryan and Katie. Ryan had to collect money every season from each team member, get the schedule, let everyone know where to be and when, and perform other management duties. Katie always hung out with the other softball wives in the stands, but she had to pay close attention to every game, as she was the official scorekeeper.

Soon they had a baby girl, and another baby girl two years later. Once again, something had to give, and in this instance it was softball. While we were all sad to see it end, we understood completely. With both of them working two full-time jobs, building a new house, and taking care of two little girls, I can imagine managing softball really began to weigh them down.

One of my hobbies is hoop dancing, which is essentially dancing with a hula-hoop. What I love about this hobby is that it's inexpensive and you can enjoy it either on your own or with others. I like to set up hoop jam sessions once a week with some friends. In the colder weather, we enjoy our sessions indoors in the gathering space of a nearby church.

At first it was only two or three people, and we kept it to the same day and time every week. But soon more women expressed interest in joining us, and suddenly I was texting people every week. And sometimes I had to change the date and time for our sessions depending on the church schedule. I soon realized I was notifying multiple people in multiple ways each week and it started to be a challenge.

Thank goodness for social media! Now all I do to let people know about our hoop sessions is post the day, time, and location each week on a certain page every Sunday afternoon. It's automatic and I post without thought, which of course is one of our key concepts for reducing mental labor.

When it comes to hobbies, always remember their purpose in your life. Our friends at Merriam Webster define a hobby as "a pursuit outside one's regular occupation engaged in especially for relaxation." That last word should serve as your guide - relaxation. If a so-called "hobby" starts to contribute to your mental labor, perhaps it's time to rethink it, scale back, and find something else that brings you both enjoyment and escape!

# Chapter Nine

## Caregiving

### Caring for an Elderly or Disabled Relative

Caregiving and its challenges in relationship to the mental load could almost be a book on its own. I know - I'm living it!

We've all heard the saying that it takes a village to raise a child. It also takes a village to care for an elderly parent. At least, that's how it should be. Doing it alone is physically, emotionally, and spiritually draining when you're in the sandwich generation.

Fortunately, we have an excellent village helping my mother. I'll introduce you to the team.

First there's the Vice President of Finances, my brother Mark, assisted by his lovely wife, Janie. Mark handles Mom's investments and pays her bills. He and Janie did the lion's share of work when we had to sell Mom's house.

Mark has also been in the insurance business for decades, so he actually understands and handles all of that insane Medicare stuff for Mom. Praise the Lord.

Next there's the Vice President of Long-Distance Observation, my sister Vicky. Vicky lives in Florida, but she calls Mom every Sunday and takes care of as much as she can when she comes up to visit. Vicky often sees the things that local members of the team miss and is a good listener when some of us (ahem, me) need to vent from time to time.

I hold the title of Vice President of Day to Day Affairs. My responsibilities include doctor, dentist, and eye appointments, groceries and OTC medication delivery. and just generally watching out for how things are going at Mom's facility. And, of course, my family and I make sure to have fun with Mom with lunches, dinners, euchre games, shopping excursions, and musical outings - her favorite!

I can't say enough good things about the next team member, Michelle, Executive Assistant to all VPs. Her other title is Angel Sent from God. Michelle is a contractor for various assisted living facilities in the area. She takes Mom for her hair appointment every Friday and runs other errands as needed. Michelle is a nurse who knows more about elderly issues than we novices, so she's quick to point out things we need to be aware of. Like most Executive Assistants, we couldn't run this operation without her. I thank God for Michelle!

Finally, there are the numerous CNAs, nurses, housekeeping members, dining room employees, and maintenance folks at Mom's facility who are so kind and thoughtful. We know they work long hours to help Mom and everyone else live happy, healthy lives. They all round out the team beautifully.

I can't appropriately express my gratitude to this entire village. I would lose my sanity without them all and am thankful I'm not alone on this journey.

But what if you're an only child or the only relative close enough to take care of someone? You still don't have to manage the mental load alone if you are caring for an elderly parent or relative. Many free or low-cost resources help make life easier.

For example, "Senior Summits" pop up often throughout the U.S. and beyond. These seminars feature topics such as Planning for Aging, Housing Options, and Caregiver Resources. You're sure to walk away with many ideas and tools thanks to these events.

Many nonprofits help seniors and their caregivers. One of our local organizations has a mission of "Promoting and supporting independent lifestyles for senior adults." It offers Community Caring, Reaching Resources, Together Today, and other programs. Organizations like these can assist you as you navigate aging issues or point you in the right direction to other organizations that can help.

Did you know there are outstanding senior centers all over the world? Many serve those 55 and over with numerous programs and resources. I've had the pleasure of working with one through my consulting business this year and have been astonished at what this all-volunteer non-profit accomplishes!

Councils on Aging are dedicated to enhancing the lives of senior residents by advocating, communicating, and promoting solutions. Their caregiver support and resources are excellent. In Central Indiana, we are blessed to have CICOA, The Central Indiana Council on Aging. Check them out at www.cicoa.org.

One national group that helps families is A Place for Mom. When we had to find an assisted living facility quickly for my mom two years ago, this organization made the process simple and less overwhelming. My brother and his wife contacted them the Friday after Thanksgiving and they were touring facilities the next day. We were able to narrow our selections quickly and showed Mom two places the following Monday. She picked out her facility that evening. You can learn more at www.aplaceformom.com.

And I can't forget Meals on Wheels where I volunteered years ago. This organization offers meal delivery to the elderly. The non-profit has locations throughout the U.S. and they help homebound seniors get the proper nutrition they need.

Hospital and Health Center Transportation Services are also terrific. In my city, patients with appointments at 29 locations affiliated with our county hospital can use this service for just $5. I haven't had to call them yet for Mom, but it's good to know it's there.

Similar organizations exist throughout the United States and beyond. Just Google "senior services" or "caregiver resources" plus your location and you'll be off and running!

I take other steps to help with the mental load of caring for my mother. I keep track of her schedule using the system I use for my family, which is currently Outlook. I use phone reminders to help me as well. I visit her every

Sunday and that's when I write down what she needs from the grocery store. I use Shipt to have her groceries delivered every Friday. I pay the annual membership fee and weekly tips for the delivery people, which is worth every penny for me. Mom even has "regulars" who know her well and look out for her!

Another essential tool for me is Amazon. We are Prime members and it has helped me in a pinch for Mom more times than I can recall.

I remember one Saturday she called me saying she was out of Osteo Bi-Flex. This happened to be a day when I was not feeling well.

I hopped on Amazon, found the type of Osteo Bi-Flex Mom needed, and chose same day delivery. Yes, I paid five dollars more for this convenience, but I felt miserable and I certainly didn't want to expose Mom to my germs. Once again, it was worth every penny.

Finally, I've learned to not be afraid to ask for help. Sometimes it's just not possible for me to drop everything, especially when I have work commitments. Thankfully, as I mentioned earlier, Mom has wonderful team members I can call on in a pinch. You may want to ask your local Council on Aging if they have a list of individuals like Michelle whom I mentioned earlier. Contractors like her can perform various tasks to help senior citizens for a reasonable fee.

What about caregivers who live with a disabled or elderly relative? I know their mental load is certainly greater than mine.

I have many friends who are live-in care partners, another term for caregivers, two of whom take care of their husbands. One man is battling cancer, while the other has a long-term disability. I sat down with both of these friends and asked them about their mental load and what they do to help lighten it.

Louise is married to Kent, who has battled a long-term disability for decades. She also helps take care of her daughter, Penny, and her two grandsons, as Penny is fighting Lyme disease. On top of this, Louise also works full time.

"With both Kent and Penny, part of their disability is cognitive," Louise said, "Their condition can change on a dime. I'm constantly thinking of multiple options – I have plan A, B, and even C. Even if I discuss plans with them, they may or may not remember."

"The information they give me may not be correct," she continued. "I've learned that I just have to be ready to make adjustments on the fly. I have to be prepared."

She went on to say that those factors could create a constant tension for her.

"I've learned to let go. I tend to be a planner – I don't like spontaneity," Louise said. "It's tempting to lay down the law and say 'this is how it's going to be.' But that doesn't work for either of them. I need to be respectful and include them in the decisions, which takes extra effort, planning, and time."

For example, Louise and Kent recently received an invitation to a relative's wedding across the country. Louise had to gently discuss the event with Kent months ahead of time to outline reasons why it wouldn't be wise for them to attend. Thanks to this approach, Kent now has plenty of time to think over the trip himself. Louise will revisit the issue in another month.

"I have to watch myself to not get impatient with him," Louise said.

At this point in the interview I nodded my head in understanding. My own patience is tested almost every week with my mother and I hear the same from other caregivers.

"Another part of the mental load is just knowing that the unknown or unexpected is always waiting. I never know when something might take a turn or when I might be needed all of a sudden. What will I do if something goes wrong?" Louise continued. She shared that it takes mental discipline to control her thoughts.

"My stress levels can get pretty elevated. I have trouble concentrating and it's hard to make plans or to make time to have fun," she said. "I don't watch anything stressful on TV, I keep things light."

I wasn't surprised to hear that she has trouble sleeping and is often trired. I asked her how she manages to do it all.

"Prayer and knowing that others are praying for me," Louise replied. "Our church is incredibly supportive."

Louise said she also works to manage her expectations, stating life is much less stressful and less disappointing when she's not expecting things to go as planned. Louise attends counseling and has a strong support network of friends both in and out of her church. She's learned to let go of what she can't control and to remember to be supportive for both her husband and daughter.

"The hardest part of all this has been admitting when I can't do it and that I need to ask for help and let someone else do it," she said, "The biggest thing that helps me is keeping things in perspective. Other people have it worse off than me. God is in control and none of these things happen behind His back."

I've never met anyone stronger than Louise, who amazes me with her incredible attitude. Throughout her struggles, she dedicates prayer time every morning to focus on God, on what's positive, and on staying thankful.

My friend Maggie is another incredibly strong caregiver. Maggie is married to Derek, who has battled cancer for over five years.

"Because I work full time, I beat myself up a lot for not being able to be there or for always being behind the eight ball on things like picking up or organizing his medication," Maggie said. "The stress of putting everything aside like cleaning or doing dishes is great. I just have to block it off."

Since Derek is alone all day, Maggie tries to focus on him when she gets home from work and the gym.

"He says, 'My life lights up when you walk through the door. When you come home, life begins.' It reminds me of the whole Mary and Martha story in the Bible," Maggie continued. "It's better to be there and be by his side than to do housework."

"Your own physical health has to be put on hold. Having to juggle all the time and setting yourself to the side is stressful," she said.

Maggie admitted that this mental load makes her irritable. Derek's illness affects the couple financially, as they have to juggle things in their budget to make ends meet and to anticipate future expenses. The couple enjoys traveling but can't do it often because of finances or unexpected detours in Derek's health. She also can't focus on friendships as much as she'd like to, although Maggie tries to meet friends for coffee or lunch on occasion.

"There are a number of friends who check in and stay in touch and want to know what's going on," she shared. "Others have gone by the wayside. People have had to be intentional with me because I can't be intentional with them. As caregivers, we're probably not going to reach out because we don't want to burden other people with what's going on in our life. I try to fill people in early on in the conversation and then we'll move past it."

Maggie struggles with anxiety and depression. She's on anti-depressants and takes a sleep aid when she needs it. Maggie relies on her faith to help her as well.

"Some weeks I'm so mad and then others I'm like 'how can I be mad at God?' Other weeks I recognize the blessings and I'm so grateful. Thankfully He's got grace and is merciful. It's made me go a lot deeper."

Maggie exercises right after work at a gym and takes a walk or a run to also relieve her mental labor.

"I'll often walk our dog," Maggie said. "Having animals is such a delight! They're so funny and a distraction. They mix it up and lighten the air."

Once in a while, she'll visit her cousin in nearby Chicago to truly get away from her stress. Her other cousin comes to visit on occasion which is comforting. Maggie also gets support from her best friend and vice versa.

Maggie's last piece of advice is to downsize your life if you're in a caregiving role.

"I'm not in my normal career," she explained. "I've taken a position that allows me shorter hours, that doesn't demand I take work home. It's low pressure and I can get away for appointments when I need to. That's huge and it's okay. It's where I should be. To have an understanding staff is huge. I love my place of work."

Maggie has her master's in social work and would eventually like to counsel others in similar situations.

Whether you're caring for someone in your home, from a short distance, or across the state or country, you don't have to go it alone. Exercise and prayer can go a long way. Reaching out to a local counselor, church, non-profit, health professional, friend, family member, God – or two or more (or all!) of these – can lighten the mental load of caregiving and bring you peace.

# Chapter Ten

## Retirement

**Retirement - Beware!**

By now I'm sure you're thinking I've lost my mind. Retirement *should be* the time of life for relaxation, freedom, and the time to do what you enjoy. The words "mental load" shouldn't even be part of the equation! However, I can't tell you how many times I hear retirees say to me "I'm busier now than when I was working! In fact I don't even know how I had time to work." Unless this is how you *want* your retirement years to be, it's important to stay on your guard, be wise with your money, and protect your time so you don't fall back into the habit of battling the mental load of your working and child raising years.

The number one topic when it comes to the mental load and retirement is finances. If you don't plan ahead and take some of the steps I mentioned in an earlier chapter regarding managing your money, retirement could be stressful. And that's the last thing this time of life should be. However, it's a reality for many seniors.

I was saddened to discover some startling statistics in a February 2018 article by the Atlantic. Older Americans were the only demographic for whom poverty rates increased in a statistically significant way between 2015 and 2016, according to U.S. Census Bureau data [40]. While poverty fell among people 18 and under and people 18 to 64 between 2015 and 2016, it rose to 14.5 percent for people over 65, according to the Census Bureau's Supplemental Poverty Measure.

---

40https://www.theatlantic.com/business/archive/2018/02/pensions-safety-net-california/553970/

The article went on to say that the current wave of senior poverty could be just the beginning. Two-thirds of Americans don't contribute any money to a 401(k) or other retirement account, according to Census Bureau researchers.

Disappearing pension plans, the recession, and wages not keeping up with inflation leading to reduced savings have all contributed to the problem. And Social Security only covers about 40% of pre-retirement income. This means more and more older Americans have no choice but to keep working.

And if you're not able to keep working, the picture gets even worse. The Atlantic article shared that in 2016, nearly half of all single homeless adults in America were aged 50 and older, compared to 11 percent in 1990.

And this isn't just a problem for people in the United States. Saving enough money for retirement is easier said than done, regardless of the language [41]. Only 38% of employees globally are habitual savers, meaning they always make sure to save for retirement, according to new research from Transamerica Center for Retirement Studies (TCRS) in collaboration with the Aegon Center for Longevity and Retirement. That's down one percentage point from last year.

A paltry 23% save for retirement occasionally, and 21% are not saving for retirement but claim they intend to do so. Six percent have never saved for retirement and don't intend to. The study polled 14,000 workers and 1,600 retirees in 15 countries.

So, what can we do to change this bleak picture? If retirement is still in the distant future for you, there's still time if you're not doing anything to financially prepare for it. I encourage you to review the earlier chapter covering finances and mental labor to get you started on some research and planning if you haven't already done so for retirement.

---

41 https://www.cheatsheet.com/money-career/best-worst-countries-retirement-planning.html/

But what if you, like many people around the world, just can't put aside anything extra right now? Or what if you're close to or already in retirement? You can choose to keep working, which some seniors do at least part time anyway to continue to sharpen their skills and their social involvement.

95-year-old Dorothy Bale is just one example of a senior citizen who has no desire to retire. In January 2019 she celebrated 25 years with the popular fast food chain, Arby's, in Holladay, Utah. I heard her story on the radio and was amazed at her spunk and delightful personality. Bale started with the company at age 69 because she was looking for something to do. She loves her part time job and everyone she comes in contact with while she's at Arby's.

Other seniors, however, aren't able to work even part time for various reasons. For those who fall into this category and are struggling financially in the U.S., the federal government, your state, Area Agency on Aging offices, and other non-profits or social service organizations offer numerous resources. To find what might be right for you, visit:

https://www.needhelppayingbills.com/html/senior_assistance_programs.html.

Hopefully, one or more of these options can help lessen the financial mental labor so many people experience during retirement. But what else do retirees face when it comes to the mental load?

More and more grandparents are raising their grandchildren. In 2012, 2.7 million grandparents had the primary responsibility for caring for their grandchildren who lived with them according to the U.S. Census Bureau. The most common reasons for this fairly new phenomenon include poverty, substance abuse, the death of a grandchild's parent and extended military deployment.

Fortunately, the federal government is recognizing this trend and supporting it. The Supporting Grandparents Raising Grandchildren Act was signed into law in July 2018. The act first established a Federal Advisory

Council to support grandparents and other relatives raising children. The U.S. Department of Health and Human Services (DHHS) is the lead agency coordinating the work of the council. DHHS will identify, promote, coordinate and disseminate information about resources and best practices to help relative caregivers meet the health, educational, nutritional and other needs of the children in their care. The agency will also help grandparents maintain their own physical and mental health and emotional well-being.

I'm thrilled to see this progress on a federal level, but I know this process won't happen overnight. I was curious about the trends in other countries. To my surprise, I found that in many Asian countries, grandparents do most of child raising duties, as many families have three generations or more under one roof. And in Spain, more than half of grandparents watch their grandchildren every day.

Unfortunately, in many instances, raising a grandchild can also cause financial hardship for seniors. Thankfully there is a plethora of resources in the United States for this situation as well, including Social Security benefits, free daycare in some areas, and Children's Health Insurance Programs (CHIP) in various states. You can see these and other options at:

https://freefinancialhelp.net/grandparents-raising-grandchildren-resources/.

Thankfully, support groups are popping up all over the United States for grandparents raising their grandchildren. I've seen many online groups as well.

The American Association of Retired Persons (AARP) has some good tips for managing the mental load when raising grandchildren. They include:
- Ask for help. Make a list of small and large ways family and friends can support you. Asking for help is a sign of strength, not weakness. It shows that you are going to do your best in raising your grandchild and you know what it will take to get that done.

- Have a family conference or meeting of close and extended family members. Discuss how your life, your grandchild's life and other family members' lives will change.
- Try to divide up tasks and responsibilities for other areas of your life, such as caring for older parents, so you can have the time and energy for raising children again. A small amount of planning can save you some big headaches later.
- Talk with your friends about how your social life will change. Let them know you'd still like to see them, but you might need help with babysitting.

Finally, you can talk to your local school system, faith-based organization, or

various nonprofits to find out how they can help you on this journey as well.

We've covered how to reduce the mental labor of finances and raising grandchildren during retirement. How about those people I mentioned at the beginning of this chapter who are just simply too busy when they may not want to be? The U.S. News and World Report summed this situation up well in a December 2016 article [42]:

"After you retire and you no longer have to go into work every day, it seems like

everything else expands, multiplies and rushes in to consume the time you used to

---

42 https://money.usnews.com/money/blogs/on-retirement/articles/2016-12-08/is-your-retirement-fulfilling-or-just-busy

work. You may wonder how you ever had time to work and still get everything done," the article states.

It goes on to say that many retirees discover their life suddenly becomes busy, but not fulfilling. To discover how to fill your days with activities that are both fun AND fulfilling, step back and examine what's working for you, what isn't, and what's missing. Find a quiet time and a place where you can be free from distraction. Make three lists labeled "start doing", "stop doing" and "keep doing".

"Think about what you want to do. Then think about what's missing from your life. Try to remember what you have done earlier in your life that brought you fulfillment. Think about what you truly value and what matters most to you," the article said.

Rewarding activities can include volunteering for your church or nonprofit; pursuing creative endeavors like painting or writing; hiking, gardening, or other physical activities; exploring nature and new places; spending time with people you love; or just enjoying books, museums, plays, and movies.

The best tip I can share to help you greatly reduce the mental load in retirement is to remember to do the things you *want* to do in life versus the things you feel you *should* do. You now have the freedom to live life on your own terms as a retiree. Chances are you've worked hard all of your life either through a career, at home, or doing both. You've done enough mental labor over the years! It may take some work to reprogram your mindset, but if you do, you'll find your retirement years will become the best ones of your life.

# *Chapter Eleven*

## Guard That Lightened Load and Don't Add to the Load of Others

**Lighter? Keep it That Way!**

Dear Readers, I hope you and I have come a long way with our mental labor. We may not have reached every goal for each facet of our lives yet, but we're implementing some new tips and tricks and sighing in relief.

I promised that I would go on this journey with you, and I'm happy to report I'm well on my way to lightening my mental load. I've stopped reminding my boys to plug in their iPads for school the next day. I no longer ask my son Jonathon for his dirty gym clothes. He is completely responsible for getting them out of his backpack and putting them in the laundry basket. If they don't make it into the washing machine when they're dirty, he just gets to be a bit smelly for his Lifetime Fitness class.

I'm gradually reminding my sons less about doing chores (not completely, but getting there). I've been saying "no" to my mother a little more often, albeit gently. Our local pharmacy now sends John an automatic reminder on his phone versus mine and he is responsible for picking up his own prescriptions. When the gastroenterologist mailed him a reminder about his colonoscopy, he put it up on the refrigerator to handle the appointment himself.

I'm still using my wonderful cleaning service, but I recently took a four-day weekend to do a serious deep clean on our house to get everything more organized. As I write this, the KonMari method of de-cluttering, deep cleaning, and organizing is all the rage around the world. I studied Marie Kondo's principles through her book and her Netflix television series before this four-day weekend. While I didn't agree with everything she says, I adopted the steps that made the most sense for our family and we all worked together to re-organize our home. We took two minivan loads of items to thrift stores, one carload of electronics to our local household hazardous waste facility, recycled two trash cans' worth of items, threw away another two trash cans' worth of trash, and shredded an entire grocery bag of papers.

Thankfully we have a new garage that is still fairly well organized, and I did a deep clean of our basement last summer. Taking all of these steps was hard work, and it left my family and me aching and exhausted. However, de-cluttering, reorganizing, and deep cleaning has greatly reduced my mental load of taking care of our household. We can all find exactly what we need much quicker, which helps our days go smoothly.

And oh, how I love our A.I., Alexa! It's funny how this Christmas gift for my husband is now an essential tool to help *me* manage various tasks. When I need to remember to let our cat back in on a frigid winter day, I just ask Alexa to remind me in 20 minutes and I don't have to worry anymore. Grocery shopping list? Alexa's got it. Do my sons have to warm up their vehicles in the morning? We just ask her to tell us the temperature. I'm just starting to explore all the ways Alexa can help our family and me. I have to say I don't ever want to go back to living without "her."

My dry erase board has a "Meal Requests" section so everyone can put down what they would like for dinner in the near future. No more complaints about what I fix, and dinner ideas don't have to all fall on my shoulders.

I just did our taxes last weekend and thanks to gradually getting all paperwork assembled and placed into various categories ahead of time, it took less than an hour working with an online program. I'm working smarter when it comes to my business by only traveling for out of town face-to-face meetings one day a week. Yes, that's one busy day, but now I have more uninterrupted time to focus on writing solid grant applications.

Both of my board of director terms will be up by the end of this year, and I've already given them notice I will not be renewing. While I have enjoyed these roles immensely, I know with my oldest son starting college in the fall that I will need more time in my schedule for expanding my consulting and writing business. It's time to make that money!

But I'm not going to stop volunteering entirely. I've decided to return to volunteer one evening a week for our local therapeutic horseback riding center. I started my grant career thanks to working for this organization years ago. Volunteering at this center when I was younger was both fun and fulfilling. My shift will take place on a weeknight, so it won't interfere with my work. I'll volunteer on a day that my sons typically work so it won't take any time away from them as well. They are only home for just a few more years now, and I want to continue to make them a priority.

Speaking of my boys, I've booked the location for my son's graduation party and I am slowly filling a box in our basement with items we will bring for display. I've marked my Outlook calendar with various steps to prepare for the party, including when to create and send invitations. This method will help me gradually prepare for the big event and it won't feel like such a weight on my shoulders.

My other son, Jacob, decided to not try out for his choir next year, so I notified the parent organization president that I would not be volunteering for his music group this coming fall. Then he decided to weeks later to try out after all. After some deep thought and examination, I decided to leave the situation as it stood. I know my future self will be grateful.

Jacob also texted me a couple of weeks ago asking that I remind him of something. Instead, I told him to set his own reminder in his phone.

I still have a long way to go and of course will always be working to improve. We still haven't downloaded the Cozi app, darn it. There are still days where I feel overwhelmed. But just knowing I have all these tools at my fingertips is a huge help. Creating awareness in my own family has been a positive experience. I'm slowly seeing my husband and sons relying a little less on me and more on their own initiative to get things done.

One of my missions will be to continue to find new ways to reduce this mental labor. I won't be perfect, and it will never be completely gone, but just understanding the term and knowing I don't have to be a stressed-out working wife/mother/daughter is amazing. I hope you feel the same way.

I beg you, now that you're thinking through and taking the steps to lighten your mental load, don't ever stop. If we don't guard our time and resources well, we can't lead the amazing life we are meant to live. We can't use every suggestion in this book and think we're all done and that our mental load won't ever grow again. Be careful dear readers - that mental labor is sneaky and will start to increase the moment we let our guard down.

But please don't just help yourself in this area. We have to make certain to not add to the mental load of others, especially women. Let me share two examples of how - I'm ashamed to say - I goofed in this area.

I remember a dear friend of mine felt upset on her birthday a few years ago. She commented that her son didn't even send her a card or make a phone call to her. I felt sad and angry on her behalf and said without thinking, "That's terrible! Doesn't he have a wife?" Yes, I'm embarrassed to say that those words came out of my mouth. What I was essentially saying is that his wife should have handled reminding her husband to send a card or call, or that she should have bought a card and sent it for him!

Bad Amy. Bad, bad, bad Amy.

Obviously, I know better now. For example, I texted my friend Kim four months ago about her sons taking care of our house and dogs so we could go to Illinois to visit my father-in-law for Thanksgiving. After she replied that they could help, I literally stopped in my tracks. Her boys are 19 and 14. They both have cell phones. Why was I adding another task to Kim's already busy schedule? She's a wife and mother who works part-time as a nurse and also volunteers often in our church.

I texted Kim again and asked her to give me both of her sons numbers so I can contact them directly in the future. She was happy to oblige. I've vowed next time to contact her boys directly, so I don't add to Kim's mental labor.

Folks, that is one of two keys to changing our society's behavior when it comes to the mental load. We have to 1. Make things better in our own lives and households and 2. Work together to help others do the same. Stop asking wives to help with planning vacations and social outings alone. Don't ask a mother about what her child can do to help you if he or she is old enough to talk or text on the phone.

Let's remove the stigma when someone hires help to clean their home or do other household tasks. Maybe your friend gets that monthly massage to help her relax and manage a chronic illness, which enables her to be a better wife and employee. Don't roll your eyes when a man says that he's got a lot on his plate. He may very well be a single working dad, or holding down a job and managing an entirely separate company.

We also have to change the division of mental labor for future generations. Gemma Hartley tackled this subject in her brilliant article featured in Harper's Bazaar in

September of 2017 [43].

"My son will boast of his clean room and any other jobs he has done; my daughter will quietly put her clothes in the hamper and get dressed each day without being asked. They are six and four respectively," she wrote. "Unless I engage in this conversation on emotional labor and actively change the roles we inhabit, our children will do the same. They are already following in our footsteps; we are leading them toward the same imbalance."

Harley shared that children learn their communication patterns and gender roles from a variety of people and institutions, but their parents are the ones that they, in theory, interact with the most. So if we want to change

---

[43] https://www.harpersbazaar.com/culture/features/a12063822/emotional-labor-gender-equality/

the expectations of mental labor for the next generation, it has to start at home.

"For parents, this means making sure that one spouse does not do more of that type of labor than the other. Speaking in terms of how emotional labor is currently divided, girls will hopefully learn not to expect to have to do that labor and boys will hopefully learn no to expect females to do that labor for them. Children watching parents share that emotional labor will be more likely to be children who expect that labor to be shared in their own lives," Hartley said.

She went on to say that she knows it's not going to be easy for her or her spouse to tackle the splitting of mental labor. Haley admitted that it might never be completely equitable, as she's more skilled at mental labor thanks to her life experience with it.

"But if we're lucky, he's got a whole lot of life left to hone his skills and to change the course of our children's future. Our sons can still learn to carry their own weight. Our daughters can learn to not carry others."

By managing our tasks better, we can set great examples for our children and others in our lives. We can show them that life doesn't have to be this constant stressed out "busy-ness." By reducing our own mental loads and being kind and watching out for the ones others carry, maybe we can all finally become our best selves and help improve our world.

It's been a pleasure to be on this journey with you. May your mental load stay light, and your joy increase!

## For More Information I highly Recommend

*The Mental Load: A Feminist Comic*, Emma. (Emma, *The Mental Load: A Feminist Comic*. New York, NY. Seven Stories Press. 2017.)

I firmly believe Emma deserves all the credit for finally defining what many of us were feeling and raising awareness of the mental load and how it's crushing people around the world. This viral comic started millions of conversations everywhere that needed to happen, and I'm incredibly grateful. While the book covers other topics outside of the mental load, its thought-provoking comics will really open your eyes to various issues women face today.

***

*The Life-Changing Magic of Tidying Up: The Japanese Art of Decluttering and Organizing,* Marie Kondo. (Kondo, Marie, *The Life-Changing Magic of Tidying Up: The Japanese Art of Decluttering and Organizing.* New York, NY. Penguin Random House. 2014.)

This resource came to me a bit late on the scene, as I didn't even know about it when I began to write this book. And while I don't agree with every single technique Kondo uses, and I'll bet I'm not alone, I think using just the tips that work for you and your own household can make a world of difference to make your life easier. One of her basic principles is storing items vertically versus horizontally. This one tip has made finding clothing, kitchen tools, and food in our pantry, refrigerator, and freezer so much easier! The book is a quick read but can make a lasting impact.

***

## Book Discussion Questions

1. What areas of life create the most mental labor for you? Did you discover some tips and tricks in this book to help you manage this labor better? What were your favorites?
2. How do you feel physically, mentally, emotionally, and spiritually when your mental labor gets out of control? Do you get overwhelmed and tired like the author?
3. Do you take steps to lighten your mental load that weren't mentioned in this book? If so, what are they?
4. Do you agree that women carry more of the mental labor than men in many instances? Why or why not?
5. How have you consciously or unconsciously added to the mental labor of others? What will you do differently from now on?
6. Do you know someone who needs help with their mental load? What are they facing that might be different from you? How can you help them?
7. Do you enjoy using technology and online resources to manage your mental load? How have either of these helped you?
8. If you have a spouse or other life partner, do they share the mental labor in your household? If not, why?

## *About the Author*

Amy Thornton Shankland, like many working wives and mothers around the globe, has battled the mental load for decades. Thanks to the discoveries she made while writing this book, she's finally on her way to winning the war and finding more joy and peace in her life.

Shankland loves to write and is a former columnist for the Noblesville Daily Times, freelance writer for Indy's Child, and editor for her church's bulletin. She also created an "Enthusiastic Mama" blog that ran from 2015 - 2016.

Shankland self-published and promoted a novel called *Hoop Mama* in 2013 through Fast Pencil and published a self-help book called *Joy to You and Me (At Work!)* through Tell-Tale Publishing in 2018.

She has given local, regional, and national workshops on various writing topics thanks to her 18+ years as a grant professional.

Shankland lives near Indianapolis with her husband, two sons, three dogs, and two cats. She enjoys volunteering for various local organizations, hoop dancing, reading, and walking everywhere she possibly can.

Twitter @AuthorThornton

Facebook @authoramythornton

authoramythornton.wordpress.com

***

Tell-Tale Publishing Group and its affiliates would like to thank you for your purchase. If you would like to read more by this or other fine TT authors, please visit our website:

www.tell-talepublishing.com

\*\*\*